Responding to Grief

Avril Rob

Liverpool John Moores University

Also by Caroline Currer

Concepts of Health, Illness and Disease (editor with M. Stacey)

Responding to Grief

Dying, Bereavement and Social Care

Caroline Currer

Consultant Editor: Jo Campling

palgrave

First published 2001 by
PALGRAVE
Houndmills, Basingstoke, Hampshire RG 21 6XS and
175 Fifth Avenue, New York, N.Y. 10010
Companies and representatives throught the world

PALGRAVE is the new global academic imprint of
St. Martin's Press LLC Scholarly and Reference Division and
Palgrave Publishers Ltd (formerly Macmillan Press Ltd).

ISBN 0–333–73639–7

This book is printed on paper suitable for recycling and made from fully managed and sustained forest sources.

A catalogue record for this book is available from the British Library.

10   9   8   7   6   5   4   3   2   1
10   09   08   07   06   05   04   03   02   01

Printed in Malaysia

Contents

List of Tables

Acknowledgements

It would not have been possible to write this book without the support and encouragement of Kate Atherton, Judy Hicks, Carol Holloway, Jenny Pardoe and Margaret Wareing and of colleagues in the Social Work Department at Anglia Polytechnic University. I am grateful too to Jo Campling for guiding me through the process, to Jeanne Katz for her helpful comments on an early draft, to librarian Thelma May and to David Oliviere for some timely help.

In researching the experience and role of social care practitioners, a number of people have given generously of their time, and it has been a privilege to hear from them about their work. In addition to those already mentioned, particular thanks are due to Graham Badger, Jane Burditt, Lyn Crisp, Grace Cunningham, Chris Davis, Judy Edwards, Julia Franklin, Leila Gordon, Dini Hardy, Carla Hodgson, Nicki Hone, Joyce Jones, Joyce MacDonald, Greg Mantle, Christina Mason, Ian Morris, Mary Pennock, Sue Percival, Valerie Peters, Jill Rapoport, Clare Seymour, Jean Swanson, Tessa Sowerby and Nick Tyndall. I trust that they will feel that the whole does justice to the parts that they will recognise.

Each year, I learn afresh from the second-year Diploma in Social Work students who take the 'Loss and Social Work' elective module. Whilst preparing this book, I invited one cohort of students to contribute examples that relate theory to practice in responding to grief. I am grateful to all those who responded, especially Jill Ahmet, Colette Boukhoufane, Lucy Firmin, Sue Foster, Fiona Flynn, Sharon Gage, Audrey Hornsey, Vic Inderjeet, Helen Jocelyn, Glenda Lanoix, Melvyn Plum, Karin Roberts, Louisa Ruff, Cherie Smith, Paula Stockwell, Marion Talbot, Jocelyn Trent and Barbara Vincent. They will recognise some of the examples given, but I hope that no-one else will. All details have been altered, and any errors are mine, not theirs.

Chapters 4 and 7 draw heavily on published accounts by dying and bereaved people of their experiences. Those of us who seek to understand these aspects of life owe much to others who have written or spoken about their own feelings and experiences. I hope that what is here does justice to the accounts from which I have quoted. Particular thanks are due to Andrew Pearmain and Richard Davies for permission to use the

Norfolk study. My work with a wide range of people in CRUSE has taught me much. I have joined the National Association of Bereavement Services only fairly recently, at a point when their future is in some question. It is my hope that by the time this book is published, that future will be more certain, as I have been impressed by the need for the work they do.

I am fortunate to have children who remind me that life is more than work, and a partner who believes in what I am trying to do, even when I lose sight of it. My thanks therefore go to Lynne, Rachel, Natalie and Alan. The book is, however, dedicated to my parents, whose support continues to be unfailing, in this as in everything.

CAROLINE CURRER

To Joy and Alan Johnson

1

Introduction: Dying, Bereavement and Social Care

Care of people who are dying falls, in most of the world, largely to informal carers – most frequently to family members. In modern European countries, the diseases that are the most frequent causes of death are slow (*Lancet* 1997), so the time between diagnosis and death may be a relatively long one. In Britain, statistics show that, for people who are terminally ill, 90 per cent of the last year of their life is typically spent in their own homes despite the fact that a majority actually die in hospital (Field and James 1993). Research has found that most people would prefer to die at home, and that it is likely to be social, as well as medical, reasons that prevent this (Townsend *et al.* 1990). In Britain, therefore, care of those who are dying is predominantly a community affair.

In the case of bereavement, little formal assistance may be seen to be needed, so long as the grieving person is capable of independent living in a practical sense. The concern of friends and relatives is usually, for the majority, now a private and personal matter, handled more or less sympathetically, often with little in the way of custom or ritual to guide its expression.

The Beveridge Report of 1942 is generally taken to be the foundation of the NHS (Iliffe 1983: 25; Moore 1993) and of a welfare state that aimed to provide care for its citizens 'from cradle to grave'. Subsequent policies and legislation have altered radically the forms of this provision, but Great Britain still has, over 50 years later, health and welfare services which account for over 25 per cent of GDP (European Commission 1998). In a mixed economy of care, health and social care services are increasingly the result of partnerships between state, private and voluntary bodies within a common legislative framework.

Within this framework, the boundaries between health and social care are often blurred; they are also changing. The very term 'social care' is relatively recent and has arisen from the need for a common term to describe welfare services that are increasingly diverse in terms of

1

organisation and funding. Similarly, 'social care worker' is a generic term that is used to describe all those who work in these services. It therefore encompasses some with a claim to professional status (social workers) as well as others who have traditionally had little, or minimal training (such as welfare assistants, care assistants, home carers). The next chapter looks more closely at definitions and at commonalties across the care sector. In what follows, the generic terms 'social care' and 'social care worker' will be used except where there is specific reference to those with a professional qualification.

Formal services for people known to be dying, and for those caring for them at home, were initially not a priority for either health or social care services in the UK, but by 1987, palliative medicine was recognised as a specialty within medicine (Sheldon 1997: 5). Palliative care – in Britain as throughout the world – has now become synonymous with specialist care for those who are dying, encompassing physical, psychological, social and spiritual aspects and extending beyond death, since the focus is on the family as well as the patient. Thus care in bereavement is part of the remit as well as care of the dying. Palliative care has an evangelical side, aiming in Britain to 'permeate the mainstream' of health and social care (Oliviere *et al.* 1998).

This book is not primarily about specialist services (although they are included too), but about that mainstream, particularly that side of it which is known as social care. Given that dying and bereavement both typically take place in the community, rather than in specialist palliative care settings, it is not surprising that those paid workers who are based in the community are frequently working with people who are either dying or bereaved. In the case of people who are dying, workers may be instrumental in providing some of the practical support that is aimed at helping them to remain at home, but this is only one example of a wide range of ways in which they may be involved. This volume seeks to illustrate this variety as it exists in both mainstream and specialist services, thus providing a general introduction to this aspect of social care and demonstrating that social care workers have a particular and valuable contribution to make in this area of work.

1.1 Dying, Bereavement and Social Care: An Ambiguous Relationship

To what extent does work with those who are dying or bereaved feature within training for social care? The answer may give us an indication of the importance that this area of work is seen to have for these workers. Promotion and regulation of training for employees across the whole sector of social care has only recently become a government priority, although professional training for social work has a longer history. A National Training Organisation (NTO) known as the Training Organisation for the Personal Social Services (TOPSS) was established in 1998 to regulate standards of training across the care sector. It subsumes the work of the Central Council for Education and Training in Social Work (CCETSW) that has, until recently, governed professional training in social work. For social workers, the current national qualification is the Diploma in Social Work. Other social care workers are expected to undertake National Vocational Qualifications (NVQs) in Social Care. We need therefore to consider the place of dying and bereavement within both the Diploma in Social Work, and within NVQs at level 3 and 4.

Within the NVQ framework, loss and change are covered at Care Level 3. This is a qualification for those likely to have some responsibility or autonomy in the day-to-day delivery of care to people with 'medium to high levels of dependence' (Care Sector Consortium 1998: xxxvii). This includes care assistants in residential, day care or domestic settings and home care organisers or managers. 'Supporting people as they die' is one of the specialist interventions that may fall within the remit of these practitioners, and a further optional unit offers training that relates to this. In this instance, dying includes the time prior to, around and after death, and family and friends are a focus of care as well as the dying person (Care Sector Consortium 1998).

Within the Diploma in Social Work, work specifically with those who are dying or bereaved receives little or no attention. The broader topic of loss and change is, however, widely seen to be essential for all in social work (Sheldon 1998; Quinn 1998) and said to be 'well covered in training' (Sheldon 1998: 1212). The absence of a specialist focus within qualifying training is not surprising since the profession has campaigned for many years for a three-year rather than two-year course. This time is barely adequate to accommodate basic material, and therefore all specialism within qualifying courses is tightly regulated. For workers across the sector, in-house training courses on matters to do with care of dying people or with bereavement may be offered by Social Services Departments and these courses may be seen as particularly important for those whose work is with older people, but this provision is not routine.

Since 1991, there has been some specialist development in certain social work courses, sponsored by the Cancer Relief Macmillan Fund, which has established six social work lectureships in palliative care. For one of these, the remit has been to set up palliative care social work as a 'particular pathway' within qualifying training (Slater and Oliviere 1997). It is fair to say, however, that outside such specialist developments at the professional end of the training spectrum, work with people who are dying or bereaved has not had a high profile within training for social care generally.

Are the needs of people who are dying or bereaved specifically mentioned in the legislation that provides the basis of social care? Two statutes are of particular significance: the NHS and Community Care Act 1990, which forms the basis of work with adults, and the Children Act 1989, which has replaced earlier legislation relating to work with children. Together these provide the structure for the majority of social care services, although other legislation relates to specific groups, and aspects of earlier legislation still apply. More detail is given in Chapter 2. Neither dying nor bereavement is specifically mentioned in either statute, although children or adults who have a disability or are seriously ill (both circumstances that may apply to some of those who are close to death) would be seen as 'in need' and therefore covered by their provisions. Dying and bereavement are not, then, highly visible in either training or legislation relating to social care, although 'loss and change' has always been central.

Yet in 1989, Philpot argued that 'the social worker has an essential place in the care of dying people and those who are bereaved' (1989: 12). Is this still the case? Lloyd (1997) reports a study of the views of social workers based in hospitals, and concludes that they do have an important part to play in the care of dying and bereaved people. Quinn reports that 'social workers who are based in locality teams, especially those in "Elderly and Disability" teams, those based in general hospitals, and in residential and day units ... frequently work with dying people, although this may well go unrecognised' (1998: 12). Sheldon confirms this (1998) and sees this area of work extending in the future. Reporting on demographic changes that have implications for those who are dying and their carers, Seale argues that 'people who currently consider themselves to be working with "the elderly" are also working with "the dying"' (1993: 53). Despite an apparent consensus, then, that mainstream social care workers *are* working with dying people to a greater or lesser extent, and that they have something to contribute, this is often not acknowledged, either by the workers themselves, or by other commentators. It is notable, for example, that sociologists who study the care of dying people rarely refer to social care workers. Most workers in social care themselves see work with dying or bereaved people as a specialist role.

There are indeed a small number of highly specialist social workers in this field. Numbers are difficult to ascertain, but are around 300–400 nationally. Of these, 264 (February 2000, personal communication) belong to the Association of Hospice and Specialist Palliative Care Social Workers whose role is that of mutual support, information and research. The remit of one of the specialist teaching posts already mentioned is to 'permeate the teaching of palliative care throughout the social work courses' rather than to establish specialist courses (Quinn 1998). From this experience, the post-holder pinpoints some of the difficulties that social workers have in applying the principles of palliative care in mainstream social care. This leads her to identify some key concepts that can underpin transfer of knowledge and skills – concepts that are covered in Chapter 3. Yet there is also a sense that social work has always been there. For example, Philpot claims that 'helping cope with loss is very much a part of the social worker's job' (1989: 12). In other words, it is not about 'grafting on' skills or expertise, but about applying in a different context elements of the social work (and the broader social care) role that have always been central. This approach is in line with historical developments. Social workers were key players in the development of palliative care services in the 1980s, presumably on the basis of existing social work skills which they found to be relevant to this area of work.

It is not always easy for the generic worker to identify with those who write from a specialist position, however. This is partly because of issues of terminology – two excellent recent texts by leading specialist social work practitioners (Sheldon 1997 and Oliviere *et al.* 1998) speak of 'psychosocial palliative care', rather than 'social work'. These texts are careful to reflect, in the way in which they are written, the commitment of their authors to a 'holistic approach to care' and to multidisciplinary teamwork. Despite little overt reference to 'social work', they do strongly reflect core social work values and principles of social work practice. In the current policy context, where interdisciplinary work is stressed at all levels, mainstream practice has much to learn from such strongly integrated work across professional boundaries. This may, however, seem an enviable and impossible dream to workers in community settings, where the structures of work seem to discourage, rather than encourage such an approach.

Many specialist workers readily acknowledge that their work rests upon the same skill and knowledge base as other areas of social work

(Sheldon 1998). Yet not all those with a social work qualification who work in this field choose to call themselves social workers; some preferring titles such as 'family support worker'. There may be many reasons for this. For some, their social work background may be understated in order to emphasise the importance of shared teamwork. Nursing has embraced 'holistic care' in a way that includes attention to psychosocial as well as physical aspects (Hogston and Simpson 1999). Instead of entering into territorial disputes, experienced specialist social work practitioners emphasise commonalties with other specialist practitioners rather than with social work colleagues. This is understandable, but can seem to leave social work and social care outside the elite specialism.

In addition, a social work qualification is not always sought in recruits to specialist services. Other workers, such as Family Therapists or Bereavement Counsellors, may be seen as having more appropriate specialist skills in some areas. The statutory social work role has changed dramatically in recent years and is seen by many to be in danger of losing the skills necessary for emotional work and/or the opportunity to exercise them (Marsh and Triselotis 1996; Lewis *et al.* 1997). This may be a further reason why some specialist practitioners identify increasingly with the specialism and decreasingly with their social work roots. Yet the trend has not all been one way. In the co-ordination of disaster response, an area involving emotional support of bereaved people and of others who have come close to death, the central role of mainstream social care agencies has been recognised (Home Office 1994).

Much of the ambiguity concerning the place of social work (and, by extension, of social care) is related to the changing boundaries of social care and to questions of definition. Chapter 2 addresses these issues. At a time of rapid change and fierce attack, boundaries become blurred. In 1982, Carol Smith could write of social work with dying and bereaved people and refer exclusively to hospital social work, which was then a distinct area of work with a recognised professional pedigree. Even hospice care, the hub of the current specialism, is hardly mentioned in her book, reflecting how rapid this development has been since that time. By 1989, the focus of the next dedicated text (Philpot 1989) is much broader, including chapters on work in hospices as well as on work in the mainstream of social care (see chapter by Hanvey, for instance). Despite differences between them, these two texts are confident about their focus. There is now much less clarity (Douglas and Philpot 1998) – hence the purpose of this book, which is outlined below.

1.2 Aims, Approach, Sources and Structure

By now, it should be clear that this book approaches the topic of social care with those who are dying or bereaved from a generalist rather than a specialist viewpoint. As an academic responsible for professional education and training in the field of social care, my concern is to introduce readers to the wide variety of ways in which social care workers are involved, through their existing work, with people who are dying or bereaved. It is the generalists who provide the framework of care. This framework needs to be informed by the latest thinking in relation to issues of dying and bereavement, and those who work within it need themselves to be able confidently to respond to grief and to dying people in sensitive and appropriate ways. For this reason, Chapters 3 and 6 outline theoretical understandings, drawing particular attention to ways in which they are compatible with values and approaches in social work and social care.

Throughout the book, I emphasise what is distinctive and, in my view, valuable about social work and social care. This is not to deny the importance of interdisciplinary working in both generalist and specialist settings. Rather, I believe that practitioners who are well informed about the ways in which they can make a valid and distinctive contribution are likely to be able to contribute a great deal to such co-operation. Sheldon makes a similar point when she says that 'team members who are confident in what they have to offer and clear about their own role will work more easily and flexibly with the overlap and blurring that a holistic approach demands' (1997: 114).

I have been fascinated to learn from practitioners that one of the distinctive features of social work is, in their view, the quality of challenge, whether to existing theoretical models or to social inequalities. Social work seems to be in danger of losing this spirit, worn down by budget cuts, policy changes, structural reorganisation and public criticism. It can be the case that advocating for the service user may be admired in theory, but is not supported in practice. We can choose to accept this or to regain this spirit of enthusiasm and challenge. Ramon (1997) speaks of social work as 'resistance'. This book does not deny the frustrations that are currently a feature of much work in social care. It does, however, argue that we retain some choice over how we work. Social care workers are in touch all the time with those who are dying or bereaved. All practitioners need a sense of confidence about their own contribution within a network of care.

The views expressed here are my own, but based upon my teaching experience, which involves visits to students and practice teachers, and on interviews with a range of current practitioners. The views of these practitioners are particularly reflected in Chapters 5 and 8, where the focus is upon current practice. The perspectives of dying and bereaved people has been taken from written accounts, including the newsletters of voluntary organisations and groups as well as from my experience with bereaved people through CRUSE – the National Bereavement Care service.

Chapter 2 is about social work and social care. Some definitions are offered, followed by consideration of the ways in which social services in England and Wales are currently structured. The chapter then identifies some of the key features or dimensions of social care.

In my title, the word 'grief' has been used to encompass both the grief that a person feels at their own coming death, and the grief felt by others at the death (actual or anticipated) of someone significant: to refer, in other words, to the emotions of the person who is dying, or facing their own death, and of those who are bereaved. As we shall see, there is a marked similarity between the emotional states as described in these two situations. Some theorists (e.g. Seale 1998) argue that this process of grieving is the same and that separation of dying from bereavement is not theoretically justified. This argument is considered in Chapter 6, when I discuss theoretical understandings of grief and of bereavement. In terms of services, there is also an argument to be made for caring for those who are bereaved as part of the ongoing care of the dying person and their family. This is the position that is taken within palliative care, where the 'unit of care' is the dying person *and* their family.

Notwithstanding these arguments, there is a division made in this text between dying and bereavement – or, to be more precise, between facing one's own death and reacting to the loss through death of someone else who is significant. In Chapters 3, 4 and 5, we look at the situation of people who are facing the prospect of their own imminent death. In Chapters 6, 7 and 8, the attention turns to those who mourn the death of someone else. In each of these sets of three chapters, the first is theoretical, the second draws upon first-hand accounts of those involved, and the third looks at services and the responses of social care practitioners. It is really only in specialist palliative care services that there is emphasis upon continuity of care across the boundary of the death event, and in which both the dying person and their carers are the focus of attention. Most other services are set up to respond to the needs of either dying or bereaved persons.

A theoretical case can also be made for this separation of dying and bereavement. It does, in fact, underpin most of the theoretical literature, which is based upon research *either* into an individual's response to awareness of their own coming death, *or* into the experience of loss of another person through death. We should note that the distinction is not related primarily to time (before or after death) but to the identity of the central actor – the person who faces his or her own death, or their carer. The concept of 'anticipatory grief' is therefore looked at in the section on bereavement, since it is the response of the survivor, not of the dying person himself, or herself. In the same chapter, we also look at the experience of those who care for someone with dementia, who are also said to be experiencing a 'living bereavement' (Gilliard 1992), even though the person has not yet died. In contrast, services for persons who have made suicide attempts will be considered alongside those for people who are dying since they are facing the possibility of their own death, even though it may not occur at all at that time. Those who survive large-scale disaster events are in a similar position, although their closeness to death has not been chosen. They are often, however, simultaneously bereaved as they may have been related to, or friends of, those who actually died. For simplicity, the social care response to disasters is, in this text, considered as a whole together with services for those who are bereaved. Following the two major sections, Chapter 9 pulls together conclusions and recommendations.

I have avoided throughout use of the term 'loved one' to describe the person who dies, preferring the rather clumsy alternative 'significant other'. This is because we need to beware of implying the nature of the relationship between griever and grieved-for. All that is necessary for grief to occur is that the deceased was significant in some way, not that they were loved (although this will often have been the case). There is evidence that those relationships that are highly ambivalent lead to 'more complicated' grief reactions (Parkes 1996).

Examples will be offered from all sections of social care: from the voluntary as well as the statutory sector, and from purchasing as well as providing services. My aim is not to claim that these examples are representative, although I hope that they will be familiar in broad outline to those practising in each area of specialism, whether it be work with older people, with those who have a learning disability or with children and families. In relation to services for people who are bereaved, I will also consider some less common initiatives and community projects in which social care workers are involved. In surveying so vast a field of services, I am aware that some have received more attention that others. This is not intended as any reflection of their relative importance, but arises from my own greater familiarity with some areas of care together with the need to be selective.

In all of this, my aims are as follows:

- To demonstrate and illustrate the wide variety of ways in which social care workers are involved with dying or bereaved people;
- To consider the distinctive nature of the social care role and
- To draw out training and support needs.

The Health Act 1999 sets up new arrangements for collaborative working, looking to the development of Primary Care Trusts. It is up to us to claim a place as part of these new arrangements if we wish to contribute to the development of health services at a local level. The same is true in relation to new areas of collaboration with education services. In working with people who are dying and bereaved, it is my claim that those who work in social care have a proud history, a distinctive perspective (Monroe 1998) and much to contribute. If we are to do this confidently, we need to be aware of current theory and research and committed to taking responsibility for developing practice. This book aims to contribute to that process.

2

Social Care

2.1 Care and Carers: Some Definitions

Social care is the term that is now widely used in Britain in government and other publications to refer to the formal or paid care offered to citizens through welfare measures and legislation. The workforce in the social care sector is about 5 per cent of the total workforce – some one and a quarter million people (DTI 1999), of whom 80 per cent have no recognised qualifications or training (Department of Health 1998: 84). In relation to those who are qualified, Douglas and Philpot (1998) argue that 'social care now encompasses a wide range of increasingly specialised professions'.

About a fifth of those who are qualified (40,000 in 1998) are professionally qualified **social workers**. Although it constitutes only a small proportion of those employed within social care in the UK, social work as a professional activity is international. Douglas and Philpot give some sense both of commonality and of societal variations when they say that:

> Social work is a product of industrialised, urban societies, dealing with the personal consequences of social dislocation. And while Britain is one of the societies in which it can earliest be identified as a discrete activity, its forms differ from society to society according to the political and social culture and historical traditions. (Douglas and Philpot 1998: 6)

This book is concerned mainly with social care and social work in the UK. Where no country is specified, examples refer to the situation in England and Wales. In this context, the purpose of social work has been defined as follows:

> The purpose of social work is to enable individuals, families, groups and communities to function, participate and develop in society.

11

...Social workers have to balance the needs, responsibilities and resources of people with those of the wider community, and provide appropriate levels of support, care, protection and control. (CCETSW 1995: 16)

This definition is helpful insofar as it points at the outset to one of the features which distinguishes formal (paid) social care from the care offered by family or friends, often described as 'informal care'. One of the central features of social work is the activity of assessing what levels of 'support, care, protection and control' (all terms which are complex and often in mutual conflict) are 'appropriate' for this individual and in the current context.

Parton argues that 'defining the nature, boundaries and settings of social work, as distinct from other practices, has always been difficult ...social work is in an essentially contested and ambiguous position' (1996: 6). Two differing comments about the activities of social workers and the function of social work are given below. They will be useful for later discussion about the relevance of social work to those who are dying or bereaved.

Social workers become involved with people who either experience distress or cause distress. (Howe 1995: 2)

Social work fulfils an essentially mediating role between those who are actually or potentially excluded and the mainstream of society. (Parton 1996: 6)

The former emphasises individuals and their feelings; the latter points to social structures and political processes. Part of what is distinctive about social work is its concern with both levels (Thompson 1997a).

In practice, it is increasingly the case in England and Wales that the terms 'social work' and 'social care' are used interchangeably. Parton, for instance, refers to 'social work, now often called social care' (1996: 11), in a chapter which shows how such changing terminology reflects important changes in the nature and configuration of services and of the role and tasks of those employed within them. In looking to identify key aspects of this work, the last few paragraphs have referred to social work, not social care. This reflects a situation in which a recent broadening of focus and terminology has not yet been accompanied by systematic analysis of commonalties and differences within the social care sector. Social care workers, including those who are professionally qualified social workers, have however been working for many years to deliver care to vulnerable people. The new training programmes for social care reflect the general ethos and types of work that have been made explicit in the past only in relation to social work. I shall therefore assume, for the purpose of this book, that the key features of the broader social care role and functions are an extension of those that have been more comprehensively discussed in relation to the narrower area of social work.

Care is itself a frequently used term, applied to both 'formal' care workers and to 'informal' carers, who are usually unpaid. Ambiguities in the use of this term have been pointed out by sociologists (Graham 1983) who have distinguished care as an emotion (we care *about* someone we love) from care as an activity whose meaning is closer to 'tending', or 'looking after' (caring *for* someone or something). It is in the latter sense that we speak of 'care workers' or 'social care', since there is not, initially at least, a personal bond between the two, although studies of home carers (Currer 1992) have shown that the development of a personal relationship is not uncommon.

Care as an emotion and care as an activity also need to be separated when we consider those known as 'informal carers' – the vast army of people who care for dependent relatives at home. Whilst most would claim to do so out of love, this is not inevitably so. The Carers (Recognition and Services) Act 1995 distinguishes formal from informal care for the purposes of defining who has the rights to benefits prescribed through the Act. Their definition of what are elsewhere called 'informal carers' is as follows:

> A carer is defined as someone who provides (or intends to provide) a substantial amount of care on a regular basis for a disabled/ill/elderly person. The carer cannot, however, be a person who provides (or will provide) the care because he or she is under a legal contract to provide it, or does so as a volunteer working for a voluntary organisation.

This refers, then, to care as an activity, and excludes those contracted, or paid, to provide a service.

Twigg (1989) has looked at the ways in which care workers regard informal carers. She outlines three ways in which the latter may be treated by workers within social service agencies – as resources, as co-workers or as co-clients. Since she conducted her research, the Carers (Recognition and Services) Act 1995 has brought in assessment of the needs of carers in their own right (being treated as a co-client). In palliative care, it is an important principle that both patient and family are seen as members of the interdisciplinary care team (co-workers) and also part of the 'unit of care' (co-clients). In practical terms, it is the case that informal carers generally are a most important resource, both in individual cases and for the country overall. Figures from the Carers National Association (1997) show that 70 per cent of carers care for over 100 hours per week, saving the state an estimated £34 billion per year (Institute of Actuaries 1998). Informal carers carry out much of the care of dying people.

Before leaving the issue of distinguishing formal from informal care, it is important to note that care workers are also likely to be informal carers in their personal lives. This has a profound influence upon their actions and approach to work situations. There are frequently occasions when work life mirrors past or current personal experience for many employees. One of the aims of training in this area of work is to encourage practitioners to be aware of the influence that this has upon them, in order that such experience can be positively used, rather than a source of unexpected or unrecognised motivations or stress.

I have already mentioned palliative care when referring to specialist health services for dying people. Palliative is a word that itself signifies care rather than cure. The palliative approach has been seen to be 'a vital and integral part of all clinical practice, whatever the illness or its stage' and something to be adopted by all professionals (National Council for Hospice and Specialist Palliative Care Services 1995). They define its principles as:

- An emphasis on quality of life including good symptom control.
- Autonomy and choice.
- A holistic approach.
- The dying person and those who matter to that person as the unit of care.
- Open and sensitive communication with patients, their informal carers and professional colleagues.

There is debate about when palliative care begins, and whether it should be available to those suffering from all life-threatening diseases. Until recently, it has been predominantly those who have cancer who have been in receipt of palliative care. The appropriateness of this is increasingly questioned (Oliviere *et al*. 1998: 199; Sheldon 1997).

These principles of palliative care overlap considerably in terms both of focus and of values with the principles of social work and social care, with the exception that the social care worker does not usually focus upon control of clinical or physical symptoms. We should not therefore be surprised to discover many areas of commonality between specialist care of dying people and social care activities in general.

2.2   Structure of Services

In Great Britain, Health and Social Care are quite separately structured. Health Care is offered through the National Health Service, which is, as its title suggests, a national service, albeit with NHS Trusts, Health Authorities and now Primary Care Trusts (Health Act 1999) operating at a local level with a large amount of devolved responsibility. Social Care is a local service. In England there are currently 150 local author- ities responsible for the running of statutory services in their locality. In addition, there are voluntary and private agencies (which may be nationally or locally administered) which make a large contribution to the delivery of social care services. The separation of Health and Social Care is an important issue, since many service users need help from both sectors. Mechanisms for co-operation have always been a matter for debate at all levels of service, and these are being strengthened (Department of Health 1997; Health Act 1999).

Within shared legislative responsibilities and requirements, Local Authorities vary considerably in the ways in which services are organ- ised. For example, the division between purchasing services and provid- ing them was introduced in the NHS and Community Care Act 1990. In some Local Authorities, this division has come to form the basis of social service structures and teams. In others it has not, although the same functions are performed. In some Local Authorities, structuring is following new patterns through the merging of responsibility for some education and social care structures, for example. Such local variation is inevitable (Department of Health 1998), and even encouraged in some respects. The complexity of social care is also enormous. Douglas and Philpot point to the existence of 'between fifty and a hundred separ- ate Acts of Parliament setting out specific social service responsibilit- ies' (1998: 24), and tell us that in the five years following 1990, there were over a hundred volumes of new government guidance issued on social care.

Despite such complexity and fragmentation, some commonalties can be identified, and these will guide the discussion here. It is common to define social care in terms of the groups for whom services are provided. This is the approach taken in the 1998 Government White Paper (Department of Health 1998: 3). Services are usually divided into services for children and services for adults. Two major pieces of legislation – the Children Act 1989 and the NHS and Community Care Act 1990 – underpin these services respectively. Additional legislation covers work with those people with a mental illness, and work with offenders. There is also legislation covering the inspection and registration function of social care.

Services for children encompass child protection and the monitoring of children believed to be 'in need' or at risk, and the care of those now known as 'looked-after children' who are in the care of the Local Authority, either in foster homes or residential establishments. There are also family support services, and youth justice services. The guardian *ad litem* is an independent person (usually a social worker) appointed by a court to represent the interests of a child and to advise the court. Agencies may have services specifically for young carers, of whom there are between 20,000 and 50,000 in the UK (Douglas and Philpot 1998: 87), caring for adult relatives who cannot care for themselves without ongoing assistance, due often to mental health problems or disability.

Services for adults are frequently called community care services, and constitute the majority of UK social services, although it is often services for children that have a higher profile. Community Care covers services to older people, to those with a mental health problem, people with a learning disability, and the 6 million or so adults with a physical disability; also those with a sensory impairment, people who abuse substances such as drugs or alcohol, and ex-offenders. Services for carers are also included in adult services, as was the case in relation to children.

In terms of the organisation of services, social work in health care settings is in an anomalous position, which has particular relevance for the current topic of social care with people who are dying or bereaved. It is perhaps ironic that this was one of the earliest settings in which social work in the UK was established. The first hospital almoner (forerunner of the medical social worker) was appointed in 1895. Until 1970, there were separate specialist professional associations and registers, which closed when the profession was unified in line with organisational changes that brought all statutory services under one Social Services Department. Until relatively recently, these large departments have been the main employers in social care. This is now changing, with increasing involvement of charitable and private agencies in the area of social care.

Social work departments have continued to exist in hospital settings, but have become increasingly separate from the hospital in terms of accountability, which has been to their local authority employers. The NHS and Community Care Act 1990 brought further changes in the way that social services deploy their staff, and now some social work departments in hospitals are closing altogether. This has resulted from changes in the health service as well as changes in social services, but it has enormous implications for the level of co-operation that is possible between the workers involved. When Smith wrote in 1982 of social work with people who were dying or bereaved, she did so on the basis of her experience as a hospital social worker, and the setting to which she refers is mainly a hospital setting. Twenty years on, the role that she discusses – of a social worker who is a key member of the clinical team – does not, in many places, exist.

Douglas and Philpot, in their book subtitled *A Guide to Social Services* (1998), allocate a separate chapter to what they call 'specialist services'. In this they include social care in a number of health-related settings which will concern us particularly in this book, such as hospital social work, and social workers in primary care and in hospices. They also include in this chapter the special role that social services have in national services and disasters, which may involve the establishment of specialist teams to deal with bereavement and trauma. Although dying and bereavement may be associated particularly with specialist services such as these, this volume draws examples from the whole spectrum of social care services. This is to support the contention that dying and bereavement are issues for *all* social care workers, although clearly the frequency of their involvement with these issues will vary widely depending on the practice setting.

2.3 Essential Features of Social Care

Another aim in this volume is to consider the distinctive nature of the social care role with people who are dying or have been bereaved. It is important therefore to try to distil certain elements that can be looked for both in practice and in theory. Given the diversity and complexity already outlined, this is not easy. In claiming certain key aspects, I am not arguing that these features are the exclusive property of one profes-sional group. This is in line with the Barclay report on the roles and tasks of social workers, where they say that 'social workers have a monopoly neither of concerns nor of solutions' (1982: 35), yet still identify features distinctive of social work. The following suggestions draw both on theory and on practitioners' views.

The definitions already given in this chapter offer a starting point. We have seen that social work concerns 'the personal consequences of social dislocation' (Douglas and Philpot 1998: 6). It is also essentially concerned with balancing the needs and resources of a person or group against those of the community, and making judgements on behalf of the state and in the context of legislation and local policies about what is an appropriate response to their situation (CCETSW 1995). To do this, the social worker must assess the individual or group and also know what responses are possible and allowable. Parton (1996: 6) also highlights this 'mediating role' in his definition. There is ongoing assessment in provider as well as in purchasing services; in social care as in social work. For all social care workers, then, a knowledge of social policy, at a national and local level, and of the social resources available (such as welfare benefits, for example) is important. This must be combined with the ability to assess need – whether this is need for services or of ongoing needs within a particular setting.

Who are the people who use social care services? 'Social services are for all of us' claims the government (Department of Health 1998: 4). This is so, but those referred to specifically include those are 'socially dislocated' (Douglas and Philpot 1998: 6) or, as Parton puts it, 'those who are actually or potentially excluded' (Parton 1996: 6). Social exclusion results from an interactive process; we know that certain categories or groups of people are systematically excluded from social life, hence the concern of social care with structural issues of race, age, gender, disability and sexual orientation. Howe's definition (see section 2.1 above), on the other hand, relates to the individual level of personal distress. Both these levels are important for social care. For social care workers, individual service users are always to be seen in a social context. Other workers, such as nurses, are increasingly moving from a previous focus exclusively upon the individual to a realisation that the individual's needs cannot be understood in isolation from knowledge of their social situation. But this social context is rarely their primary focus. For the social care worker, the social context, and structural matters that relate to it, has always been fundamental aspect of their work. This aspect is not only true for generic workers in community settings, but is also emphasised by Monroe (1998) in her account of the specialist social work role in palliative care. For this reason, sociology and psychology are together important aspects of the theory base for social care.

What do practitioners say is distinctive about their work? All those whom I have asked have stressed the duality of practical assistance and emotional support. Unlike the counsellor, who offers intervention at the emotional level alone, or the nurse, for whom emotional support is typically combined with physical care, the social care worker offers a combination of the practical – in relation, for example, to matters such as advice on benefits – and the emotional. It is the combination of these, often in differing quantities as the work progresses, that characterises social work and social care. In order to properly assess need and either identify an appropriate response or themselves offer that response, the practitioner must understand emotional states and reactions as well as practical needs, and likewise offer a response at both levels. Again, this is as true of specialist roles (Monroe 1998) as it is of generic social care.

People who are dying and people who are bereaved both experience and (in some cases) cause distress. Dislocation, whether individual or social, is an apt term to use for their experience. Both dying and bereaved people are also, as we shall see, excluded from society in many ways, albeit (in the case of those who are bereaved) on a temporary basis. In terms of their needs, these are both emotional and practical, and it is notable that it is in palliative care – the medical specialty that focuses upon those close to death – that the importance of the family or social unit has been most emphasised. It would seem therefore that social care workers should have a valuable contribution to make to this area of work. It is my aim in what follows to demonstrate that this is the case across the whole range of social care settings outlined above.

2.4 The Social Context of Social Care: Current Issues and Trends

Personal social services are inevitably a complex product, not only of ideals, but also of their social context, in terms of time and place. In both areas, we can see examples of both continuity and change; of parallels between services in Britain and elsewhere; between services now and in the past – and of great differences.

Ideas and forms of 'community' – so fundamental to social care policies and practices – differ greatly between societies. Chamberlyne has, for example, contrasted aspects of the informal care systems in East and West Germany. She concludes that the 'caring biographies and caring strategies' (which underpin the respective welfare systems) are markedly different, 'framed by the particular social conditions of the respective societies' (1998: 133). In West Germany, she found a 'pull into the home' in caring situations that resulted, for example, in families moving house to gain more space to accommodate services and carers coming into the home. In East Germany, house moves were for the purpose of improving access to external services. This vivid contrast is an important reminder that social care is premised upon very different foundations in different places. Within Britain, a colleague gave an example of care for a person in a village situation that depended upon neighbours observing the time at which her partner left the house, and timing their contribution to her informal care around his departure. This would not occur in many urban settings. People's experiences of dying and of bereavement – and the nature of formal care services – rest upon differing foundations in different places. Staying for a moment with the European context, we can see commonalities as well as difference. The dual orientation of social work as 'servant of the state' and as 'advocate of the people' is common in many societies, and within both communist and capitalist systems (Lorenz 1994).

In social work there has since the start been a tension between care and control. Similarly, the balance between emotional and practical care has also been an issue at different times in the history of social care. In 1982, Barclay suggested that 'to many, it may seem strange that we consider we need to justify the direct counselling role of social workers... we believe it is essential that social workers continue to be able to provide counselling... such work is always part of assessment' (1982: 41). Current research (e.g. Marsh and Triselotis 1996) indicates that an allegiance to social work as an holistic activity, in which emotional issues and needs are an important component, belongs to new recruits as well as to more experienced workers. In many settings, however, workers say that assessments are being stripped of this counselling element and reduced to a 'tick-box' exercise.

Social and political contexts influence, then, the weight given within the mainstream of social care to the elements within these two key dualities that characterise social care. One difference between social work within specialist palliative care settings and in the mainstream of social care lies in the existence, in the former, of a shared philosophy and a context that emphasises the importance of emotional support. This focus was hard won by pioneers (including social workers) within a medical culture that emphasised cure, not care. It can underpin and facilitate co-operation between workers from different disciplines. Interdisciplinary working is also a policy goal in mainstream community services, and can work well where individuals have been in post long enough to develop good working relationships. Too often, however, the confusions that result from frequent structural changes have worked against close co-operation, and organisational structures and emphases have threatened, rather than supported, these stated goals.

Victor argues that 'the provision of care to dying people and their carers illustrates most of the key issues confronting the health and welfare systems in Britain' (1993: 62). What are these issues? There is a move to greater regulation and consistency though the introduction of national standards in training across the social care sector (Care Standards Bill 1999). At the same time, we are seeing an end to the dominance of local authority departments as employers. Increasing demands on health and welfare services, due in part to demographic changes, have for some time been pushing a search for demonstrated efficiency and effectiveness in both health and social care. There is a swing back towards specialism in both the health and social care sectors. New structures (such as Primary Care Groups and Trusts) offer opportunities for different ways of working across professional boundaries. In the following chapters, we explore the response that social care workers are making in situations where service users are dying or bereaved. It remains to be seen, however, whether the responses described can be supported and flourish within mainstream social care in the future.

3

Understanding Death and Dying

3.1 The Relevance for Practice of Theoretical Understandings

Spiritualists believe that it is possible to have direct communication with those who have died and are now in another place (Beloff 1993). Tibetan Buddhists believe in reincarnation and spend many years searching for the person whom they believe to be the reincarnation of a particular spiritual leader (His Holiness the Dalai Lama 1962). A popular song assures us that even after tragic death, 'the heart does go on' (Jennings 1997, love theme from the film *Titanic*). Even within one religious tradition, there may be differing views: for example, one tradition within Christianity sees it as desirable to pray for those who have died; another does not, although their lives may be remembered with thanks. These examples are sufficient to illustrate the extent to which the meaning of death is a familiar question, the answer to which has differing potential implications for continuing relationships between the living and the dead. Little surprise, then, that people's particular ideas about death influence their experience of dying. It is not only in work with those whose cultural or religious background differs from our own that we must, as practitioners, take account of the context of their understandings – this is a prerequisite for all our work.

Cultural and religious beliefs are, then, amongst the many factors that influence the ways in which people face awareness of their death. Yet they are often left out of account except in relation to 'minority groups'. This chapter presents an overview of theoretical understandings in relation to death and dying, drawing upon both sociological and psychological understandings. Much of the work in this area has been dominated by an individualistic psychological focus. Work that relates to individuals and their emotions has perhaps seemed more relevant for practitioners than the concepts identified by sociologists and anthropologists from studies of institutions or of whole societies. With Quinn (1998), however, I see some of these other theoretical contributions as particularly useful for those in social care, given the dual orientation already identified as characteristic of this work. Psychological contributions that focus upon emotional responses in people facing death are also introduced and explored.

This chapter, and Chapter 6 (which looks at theoretical understandings relating to grief and bereavement) are based on the conviction that theoretical knowledge is essential for the social care practitioner, whatever their role. This is for two reasons. Firstly, we have a duty to service users to ensure that our interventions are based upon more than good intentions. Secondly, such understanding can offer the practitioner himself, or herself, a basis for reflection upon their own practice – a way of standing back and seeing their own work critically and in context. Such reflexivity has always been highly prized in social work, as it is now in other caring professions, such as nursing (Douglas 1999). In practical terms, it protects against over-involvement and burn-out as well as offering routes to improvement of what we do.

Many practitioners and students express concern that theoretical understandings can become prescriptive. This can undoubtedly happen if frameworks are not used critically and creatively. We need to ensure both that the models we use are as broadly based and integrated as possible (Quinn 1998) and that, as practitioners, we 'sit *very* lightly' to expert understandings and models 'in order to take this one individual seriously' (Walter 1994: 119). There is a world of difference, however, between this 'sitting lightly' and the practitioner who lacks any guidance other than their own presuppositions and assumptions.

There is enormous scope for us to comment upon the appropriateness of theoretical understandings to a wide range of diverse practice situations. Some practice innovations in social work have been ahead of theoretical understandings. In relation to children's experiences of loss, for example, tools such as memory boxes, memory books, and games have been developed (the children's charity Barnardo's has a range of such products). Sadly, however, we have also often failed (in some services for older people, for example) to systematically put into practice in the services we offer even some of the most basic of the principles to be found in the literature (Siddell, Katz and Komaromy 1998).

As the subject of study, social care is also largely absent from many of the debates – at least in the UK. Thus Seale speaks of the way in which nursing has claimed 'special expertise in psycho-social care' (1998: 115).

This is indeed an area of work which is, in specialist settings, not the exclusive domain of any one professional group, as social work authors themselves point out (Sheldon 1997; Oliviere *et al*. 1998; Monroe 1998). It is one that owes much to a social work tradition, however. Despite this, sociologists who study palliative care and services for dying people seem to regard social care workers as very marginal players. There is an opportunity to remedy this. Seale goes on to argue that 'we need to see how the people who work in these settings think about their work' (1998: 117). This should surely include looking at the views and experiences of social care practitioners.

3.2 Defining Death: Biological and Social Death

Deciding the moment of physical death has been an issue within most societies. The twentieth-century explosion of medical technology has, however, made shared definitions across the world a necessity, in order to agree ethical guidelines for matters such as organ donation and transplant (Lamb 1991). Brain-stem death has been accepted as an international standard, but the application of any standard to individual cases inevitably brings ethical questions, which often hit the newspaper headlines. Related ethical dilemmas concern the right of the individual to choose to die or to limit the treatment that they wish to receive – living wills are a practical expression of this, with which some practitioners are familiar. Also familiar for some are questions of the rights of relatives to take action when they believe that the quality of life of someone who cannot choose is fundamentally compromised. Two examples of the ways in which such issues can arise in practice settings are given below.

■ A practitioner held the body of a child with a severe disability for two hours whilst his parents discussed whether or not to call the ambulance to admit him to hospital yet again, only to restore a life which would inevitably end during or after one such attack.

■ An experienced hospital practitioner reports an increasing number of older patients in hospital asking 'Can't they just give me a tablet?'

In relation to the second example, Seale and Addington-Hall's work (1994) explores the reasons why both dying people and their relatives sometimes express a wish that they had died sooner. Of particular relevance to social care is Seales's subsequent argument (1998: 190) that older women are likely to be particularly vulnerable to pressures to choose early death should euthanasia become legalised. There is therefore a direct link between this issue and questions of anti-oppressive practice.

Reflecting upon the importance of accurate diagnosis that life is extinct, a hospital chaplain reported that in his experience many are fearful of a situation in which they might be treated as dead before they are. He cited as evidence the common experience of 'hearing' a deceased relative knocking from within a coffin, and also the instructions sometimes left to solicitors requiring that a main artery be severed before interment or cremation. This phenomenon is not new. There is evidence in certain cemeteries (e.g. old Highgate cemetery, London) of mausolea with bell towers with a connecting wire through into the coffin to enable the allegedly deceased person to ring the bell in the event of waking. In a less literal sense, the experience of 'being treated as dead before you are' describes well one aspect of the experience known as 'social death'.

For those used to thinking of death as a single, biological event, the concept of 'social death' may be a new idea, but it is one with which most social care workers are, in practice, familiar. As Seale states:

> The material end of the body is only roughly congruent with the end of the social self. In extreme old age, or in diseases where mind and personality disintegrate, social death may precede biological death. Ghosts, memories and ancestor worship are examples of the opposite; a social presence outlasting the body. (Seale 1998: 34)

The concept of social death was developed by sociologists Glaser and Strauss (1965, 1968) and Sudnow (1967) who conducted studies in hospital settings in America. Sudnow defines social death as a situation where 'a person is treated essentially as a corpse, though perhaps still "clinically" and "biologically" alive' (1967: 74). He found that people who were regarded by staff as socially dead (on the basis of social characteristics such as age or economic status) were likely actually to die sooner. Timmermans (1998) has confirmed that this is still true. Glaser and Strauss also found that expectations of death determined the actions of hospital staff (1968).

Reviewing and extending the concept of social death, Mulkay and Ernst (1991) suggest that:

> The defining feature of social death is the cessation of the individual
> person as an active agent in others' lives. (Mulkay and Ernst 1991: 178)

Social death is a feature of a relationship and of how one person
perceives another; it is possible to be socially dead in the eyes of staff,
but not of a relative, for example. It is also seen as the 'final event in a
sequence of declining social involvement that is set in motion either by
participants' collective preparation for, or by their collective reaction
to, the advent of biological death' (Mulkay and Ernst 1991: 180).

The concept has been applied both to perceptions of entry to residential care, and to what occurs within them when a resident is close to
death (Mulkay and Ernst 1991). Field (1996) cites a study that uses the
concept in relation to those who develop AIDS, and may, in some
instances, experience consequent rejection and stigmatisation. Sweeting
and Gilhooly (1997) have looked at its application to the situation of
people caring at home for someone with dementia. They distinguish
believing that someone is socially dead from *behaving* towards them as if
this were actually so. Their respondents did not find the concept strange
or shocking, and a majority did believe the person they cared for was
'socially dead', but only a few treated them in this way.

This concept of social death may help us to understand some of the
differences between the experiences of those who die at a comparatively young age from diseases such as cancer, and the experience of
older people. In hospice care, there is an emphasis upon 'living until
you die'. For many older people, it can be argued that the sequence of
social withdrawal has already begun before their final illness. Residents themselves, relatives or staff may view entry to residential care as
a form of social burial: care staff have been reported as referring to
their places of work as 'God's waiting room' (Shemmings 1996: 59).
This can lead to various forms of resistance, both to entry to residential care (Seale 1998: 156) and within homes. The ways in which would-
be residents and their relatives perceive institutions are as important
as the regime that is actually in place. I consider below, in Chapter 5
(section 5.1.3), the need for those conducting community care assessments (as well as for staff in residential homes) to be aware of such
perceptions.

Defining death is not therefore merely an abstract or academic
matter. Biological and social death need to be distinguished, and the
social care practitioner will often come across people for whom these
issues throw up painful ethical questions which affect action in everyday
situations.

3.3 The Demography of Death

What is the life expectancy for different groups in society and which are the main causes of death? Some current statistics are given in Tables 3.1 and 3.2. Such facts affect the ways in which any particular death is socially understood; for example, infant deaths used to be much more common in Britain than they are now; this actually alters the ways in which the event is experienced by those whose baby dies. There is in every society, a distinction made between timely and untimely deaths; those that are to be expected and those which are not, and this affects both individual responses and the services on offer.

Table 3.1   Deaths in given age bands, as a percentage of all deaths, by gender, England and Wales, 1998

	Under 28 days	*28 days– 19 years*	*20–64 years*	*65–74 years*	*75–84 years*	*85 years +*	*All over 65 yrs*
Male	0.5	1.0	20.3	25.0	34.1	19.1	78.2
Female	0.3	0.6	11.3	16.1	32.6	39.0	87.8
Both	**0.4**	**0.75**	**15.6**	**20.4**	**33.3**	**29.5**	**83.2**

Source: *1998 Vital Statistics,* Office for National Statistics
© Crown Copyright 2000.

Table 3.2   Selected major causes of death, as a percentage of total deaths in each age group, England and Wales, 1998

Cause	*28 days– 19 yrs*	*20–64 yrs*	*65 yrs +*	*All ages, over 28 days*
Neoplasms	11.2	38.4	22.7	25.1
Diseases of the nervous system and sense organs, including motor neurone disease, Alzheimer's disease meningitis, epilepsy	10.6	2.4	1.6	1.8
Diseases of the circulatory system	4.7	29.5	43.5	41.0
Diseases of the respiratory system	7.7	6.8	18.1	16.2
Congenital Anomalies	10.0	0.5	<0.1	0.2
External causes of injury and poison	29.9	10.6	1.3	3.0

Highlighting indicates percentages over 10 per cent in any category.
Source: *1998 Vital Statistics*, Office for National Statistics
© Crown Copyright 2000.

From Table 3.1, we see that in England and Wales, the majority of people are over 75 years when they die. Death in childhood (here defined as between 28 days and 19 years) and death under 28 days old together account for just over 1 per cent of the total, and between the ages of 20 years and retirement age, deaths are just under 16 per cent of the total. Gender differences are apparent across the life span.

Looking at cause of death (Table 3.2), neoplasms (cancers) account for about a quarter of deaths in the UK, and diseases of the circulatory system for just under a half (41 per cent). This table excludes deaths under 28 days old, and those causes accounting for less than ten per cent in any age group. Thus deaths related to AIDS are not given. There are, in any case, further complexities in relation to how these deaths are recorded, and some may be listed under other causes.

'Different causes of death involve characteristic patterns of bodily events which have different implications for participation in social life' (Seale 1998: 39). Thus whilst cancer may involve relatively high levels of physical and mental distress, the period of dependency is usually relatively short. In the cases of both cancer and AIDS, death is medically predictable (although the precise timing is not), unlike heart disease. Circulatory disease, which includes heart attacks and strokes, results in sudden and unpredictable death in a significant proportion of cases. Others who have had early signs of heart trouble may live for a long time in the awareness that death is a possibility but far from a certainty. Alzheimer's disease is different again, often involving steady decline and loss of mental capacities, and a long period of dependency. This is most commonly associated with old age. Dependency is a source of fear for many people, as is pain.

These facts should be borne in mind when considering the experience of dying. As we shall see, much attention has been paid, both in theory and in the development of services, to those who die at an early age, and to those who die from cancer. This is explored in more detail below (section 3.7). Gender, class and ethnicity influence death and dying. The figures in Table 3.1 include gender as a variable, and the greater longevity of women is observable in any residential care home. The influence of social class is less obvious, but very real nonetheless: a professional person has two and a half times more chance than a manual worker of reaching retirement age, in statistical terms. Gender and ethnicity are aspects considered in a text edited by Field, Hockey and Small (1997).

Thus the social distribution of death has consequences for the way in which individuals experience death. Contrary to common myth, death is not a 'great leveller'; we must pay as much attention to issues of difference and their impact in this area as in any other. Particularly, we need to look critically at theoretical understandings and models and at the research upon which they are based. It is not that this research is not valid, but that it is necessarily specific to particular groups and their experiences – much of the early work on bereavement was based upon studies of white widows, for example. It therefore incorporated unstated aspects of gender, sexuality and sexual orientation, as well as culture. The focus of practice development and theoretical writing upon those who are aware of their coming death, rather than upon older people, who make up the majority of those who die, is a further example of such potential bias.

3.4   Changed Social Understandings of Death

The subject of death has, over the past 20–30 years, become of enormous interest to writers from many traditions – a 'revival of death' as one author argues (Walter 1994). For some time prior to this, anthropologists have reported on how the funeral rituals of other societies reflect different assumptions and meanings concerning death (van Gennep 1960; Turner 1969), and this tradition continues (Eisenbruch 1984; Rosenblatt *et al.* 1976; Rosenblatt 1993, 1997). Historians have focussed upon changes over time within Western societies (Gorer 1965; Aries 1974, 1981). Various sources of evidence, such as gravestones and memorials (Hope 1997; Rugg 1998) or records of disputes over wills (Hallam 1996) provide a basis for comparisons over time. Sociologists have been interested in such shifts as evidence of the ways in which meanings are socially constructed (Walter 1994; Seale 1998).

Walter (1994) has seen both the burgeoning interest in the subject of death and this sense of the relativity of our own understandings as themselves features of a current context – one which is often described as 'post-modern' (or 'neo-modern' in Walter's own analysis). He offers a thought-provoking analysis of the characteristics of three contrasting 'types of death', which he describes as the traditional, the modern and the neo-modern. This analysis seeks to sum up the characteristic features of death and dying in each period, from matters such as life expectancy, to beliefs about the cause of death and the ideal funeral (1994: 48). In relation to the meaning of death, he argues that while this was at one time imposed by religious authorities, it has now become, in the West at least, a matter to be negotiated or created, often on an individual basis.

Authority concerning death and dying has, in Britain, passed over time from the church (with priests as key figures) to medicine (the doctor as the 'expert') to the 'psi-sciences'. Counsellors and the dying persons themselves have become the experts concerning how to die well.

Whilst Walter offers an overall description and classification of shifts in ways of understanding and responding to death, Seale's project is to set this within a theoretical framework, which draws upon the work of Giddens (1991). This is outlined next, and will form the basis of subsequent analysis.

Death is defined as a 'falling from culture' through 'severance of the social bond' (Seale 1998: 149). The argument is that the creation and maintenance of identity are an ongoing project for us all; life is a continual turning from death. Social interaction involves ongoing and continual 'deaths' or rejections by others. The maintenance of a sense of ourselves is an ongoing project in which we are all involved all the time.

Giddens argues that consciousness is divided into the practical and the discursive: the first is about everyday habits and routines, and assumptions on the basis of which we continue most of our life. The second is about reflection and justification, which we turn to when asked or required to explain what we do. The basic routines we have offer a sense of 'ontological security' – which is a form of self-confidence or feeling safe in the world. In Chapter 6, when we look at bereavement, we will note the close links between these ideas and those of Marris (1986) and Parkes (1993).

Since consciousness is embodied, we have routines for management and presentation of the bodily self. This applies at all ages, and is perhaps as clearly seen in the behaviour of a teenager as that of their grandparent – for different reasons both may spend a long time in the bathroom creating a presentable self before venturing out. Chronic illness disrupts taken-for-granted assumptions about ourselves and imposes physical restrictions. This is a common feature of ageing. In old age, management of a body which is perhaps no longer reliable or trust-worthy, and which can offend social conventions unexpectedly, can become a major preoccupation. In France there is a definition of health which translates literally as 'to feel well in my skin' (d'Houtaud and Field 1986), conveying the sense that the physical and the social selves are not always coterminous. Young people did not choose this as a way of defining health, but older people did, perhaps suggesting that such separation becomes more apparent later in life. Seale's analysis helps us to understand what occurs when a person's body is failing, which has relevance both for dying following diagnosed terminal illness and for dying following the steady deterioration that is characteristic of the ageing process, as we shall see.

This theoretical discussion may seem a long way from our purpose, but it is very relevant to the understanding of 'social death', introduced earlier. It provides the theoretical underpinning for Seale's argument that all cultures offer to individuals a range of 'scripts' for behaviour in social situations, such as dying or bereavement. Often one such script is dominant or culturally preferred. This is the basis for his contention that medicine and the psychologically based 'revivalist discourse' on death (a concept taken from Walter's characterisation of neo-modern approaches to death) each offer distinctive 'scripts' to those who have a defined disease and can enter the 'aware dying role'. The relevance of this for practice will be drawn out below. Identification of the importance of practical habits and routines as an aspect of consciousness, together with reflexivity, seems also to validate an aspect of experience familiar to care workers. Here is a duality that seems to offer parallels to that inherent in social care.

3.5 Rites of Passage

Anthropological analyses have seen death as a major transition, and looked at the rites of passage that are associated with it (van Gennep 1960; Turner 1969). These have also been used to explore and explain some of the current practices surrounding death and dying in our own society (Littlewood 1993; Froggatt 1997). Rites of passage are sets of customary behaviour that are seen at times of major life change or transition, such as birth or death. Typically, these rites have three parts or phases. These were described by van Gennep as separation, transition and incorporation. In relation particularly to bereavement, Littlewood (1993) looks at how bereaved persons first separate from others, then experience a transitional phase before incorporation back into the 'world of the living'. Froggatt (1997) concentrates on the middle phase of transition or 'liminality' and considers how hospices offer dying people a distinctive space in which relationships are significantly different from those in society as a whole, a feature of this transitional phase in traditional societies. Littlewood identifies this same phenomenon in communities bereaved through a shared disaster; barriers are broken down as people relate as equals for the time following such an occurrence.

Separation of residents in care homes when they are seen to be near to death is a common occurrence. Froggatt (1998) describes a 'transitional category' of 'being poorly' which in the nursing homes she studied indicated deterioration in physical state, a change in the care routine and often some separation, although not necessarily a change of room, as Hockey (1990) had described. A care worker from a local authority residential home cites the following example of the way in which a man's death was handled.

■ Bob was 75-years-old, with a daughter who lived some way away and so could not often visit. He had lived in the home for six years and had no other visitors from outside the home. When his death was thought to be near, he was separated from other residents and took all meals in his room. No information was passed to the others about his state, nor asked for. They did not visit him. This was described as usual practice in that home when someone had entered their room to die.

We can see that some of the work relating to rites of passage and rituals might well have parallels with the ways in which death is handled in institutional settings. This is a reminder that changes to institutional practices may be difficult to introduce. At a cultural level, ideas of how to handle death and dying are embedded in shared norms of right and wrong behaviour that may not be consciously realised.

3.6 Dying: Introduction

By asking how people define themselves – or are defined by others – as dying, we are directed towards certain practice settings as ones in which social care workers will frequently be working with those who are facing death. Theoretical identification of 'the dying' with those who have a terminal diagnosis has led to a focus upon the experience of some at the expense (in terms of our understanding) of others. It is perhaps no coincidence that those who are neglected are those who are not seen as socially 'valued': older people and some people with a lifelong disability. Public interest in the psychological journeys and emotional states of the relatively young and articulate is not mirrored by a concern for the social inclusion of older people living and dying, often alone, 'in the community'.

Similarly, social work posts in hospice settings are highly prized. Hospice social work is seen as an elite specialism within social work, yet social work students do not show a preference for work with older people (Jack and Mosley 1997). Home carers and residential care staff are often untrained and poorly paid, and recruitment may be difficult. Such difference is explained, in part, in terms of the analysis already presented in section 3.4, of a current spirit of revival in relation to death – or, at least, in relation to those deaths which allow entry to the 'aware dying role'. The cultural 'script' for this role is informed largely by the theoretical understandings that I will describe briefly in the following pages, which have dominated work in this area for some time.

3.7 Who is Dying?

Dying concerns the time before death – but how long before? We are all dying, from the time of birth. For most of us, however, this fact does not affect daily life until something brings it powerfully into consciousness. Bereavement is itself one such event, which can bring awareness of our own mortality. In old age, the frequent deaths of those we know – perhaps of people we were at school with – make this general awareness one which is more personally threatening and immediate, but even so, it is not common to refer to oneself as 'dying' without a more specific reason. It is the medical diagnosis of the actual presence of a terminal illness that transforms awareness of general mortality into a present reality.

Even when terminal illness is present, however, two further issues are relevant. Firstly, as already noted, causes of death vary in the extent to which they offer ability to predict the course of the illness and therefore the degree of certainty with which death may be predicted. Secondly, the presence of a medical diagnosis of illness that is terminal is not the same as the person's own awareness of it. The first of these issues links with the concept of a 'dying trajectory', and the second with the theory of 'awareness contexts'. Both of these theoretical concepts were originally developed by Glaser and Strauss (1965, 1968).

A dying trajectory is the perceived course of an illness. In relation to the prospect of dying, 'the matter of certainty and uncertainty is of utmost importance' (Strauss *et al.* 1984: 66). Predictability affects the dying person, and both informal and formal carers in ways that are familiar to all in social care. For example, it has practical consequences in terms of eligibility for certain benefits and in relation to relatives' planning of the time they might need to take off work, or if and when they should visit. At an earlier stage in an illness, it might affect a son or daughter's ability to offer to have a parent living with them. In residential homes, as we shall see in Chapter 5, predictability is a key factor in whether or not deaths in the home are seen as 'easy', and affects whether a deteriorating resident is able to die in the home or has to go to hospital. Glaser and Strauss (1965) outlined four possible 'dying trajectories': certain death at a known time; certain death at an unknown time; uncertain death but a known time when the question will be resolved; uncertain death and an unknown time when the question will be resolved. These categories refer primarily to medical uncertainties. Although these categories may be hard to apply in particular instances, they do draw our attention to the variability in types of certainty surrounding medical diagnosis. Quinn (1998) suggests that they are helpful for social work students insofar as they underline the fact that uncertainty is a feature of many dying situations, in specialist as well as mainstream settings.

Even when a condition is recognised to be terminal by the doctor, the patient is not always aware of this. There is evidence, however, that over the last twenty or thirty years there has been a considerable increase in the numbers of people who know that they are dying (Seale 1991; Hinton 1994). But 'knowing' is not necessarily a straightforward matter. Glaser and Strauss's theory of awareness contexts relates to this issue. Awareness contexts are defined as follows:

> What each interacting person knows of the patient's defined status, along with his recognition of the others' awarenesses of his own definition. (Glaser and Strauss 1965: 10)

Again, Glaser and Strauss suggested four categories, shown below.

- *Closed awareness*-the dying person does not know and the person is certain of this.
- *Suspicion awareness*-the person suspects what is wrong but does not verbalise this.
- *Mutual pretence awareness*-both know that the other knows but do not acknowledge this to each other.
- *Open awareness*-the dying person and the other both know and acknowledge it openly to each other.

Timmermans (1994) has suggested that this framework emphasises rational aspects of 'knowing' and fails to pay attention to emotional processes. On the basis of his own personal experience of his mother's terminal illness, he suggests that 'open awareness' should be subdivided into three categories. These are:

- *Suspended open awareness*, where the patient is told but chooses to disregard the information (this may be a temporary initial reaction or longer term).
- *Uncertain open awareness,* in which hope is more important than certainty, so the patient or family pick and choose within information given, despite 'knowing' the worst.
- *Active open awareness,* accepting the full implications and acting accordingly.

Outside specialist palliative care settings (and often also within them), patients are frequently not fully aware of their terminal condition. However, although open awareness is seen as desirable and is a characteristic of these settings and of what one author referred to as the 'happy death movement' (Lofland 1978, cited by Field 1996), we can see from Timmermans' suggestion that even this is not a straightforward matter. In Quinn's view (1998), the concept of awareness contexts can help reduce the dichotomy that seems to exist between specialist and generalist settings, by helping us to see the complexities that exist within a question such as 'does the patient know?'

Awareness of dying forces a change in the assumptions that we have about the future. Although the person living with such a diagnosis may indeed live longer than another who has had no such warning, it is this changed orientation and way of being in the world that marks the former as 'dying'. In the later stages of illness, physical changes are likely to make this awareness one that cannot be avoided, and such changes begin to impose a completely different structure and timeframe on to the life that remains (Young and Cullen 1996).

If we ask first, then, who is dying, the clearest category must be those people who have a disease that they know to be terminal. As a consequence of medical advances, it is now possible for people to know that they are dying whilst they lead full and active lives, with little sign of sickness. Some may have a condition that is known to be eventually terminal, but in which the prognosis is so extended as to make it quite possible that they will actually die of something else first. Nevertheless, diagnosis of certain conditions (such as cancer) is, for many people, synonymous with a death sentence. Even when death is not a consequence at that time, they may see themselves as 'dying'. Definition in palliative care is based upon the presence of disease that is 'not responsive to curative treatment'. The first category of persons who can be called 'dying' are therefore those who know that they have a disease for which no further treatment is possible.

This definition of those who are dying includes some children, although their numbers are, comparatively, not great. If we look at the figures for cause of death in those between 28 days and 19 years (section 3.3 and Table 3.2, p. 27), we find that external causes such as accidents or poisoning account for a relatively high proportion – nearly 30 per cent of deaths in this age bracket. Such deaths are likely to be sudden and unexpected. 'Dying' does not therefore apply in such cases. Some children are, however, seriously sick or have a profound disability from birth or early childhood. Whilst these children are most likely to be cared for in medical settings, there are other service settings where early death is a constant likelihood. This is so in residential care settings for children with a profound disability.

To include in our definition all those who are in fact dying, whether or not they had specific warning of this, we need to work backwards from the fact of death. This was the approach taken by Cartwright and Seale (1990) in their research concerning experience during the last year of life. Of course, this means that the only people who can be asked to comment are those who knew the person who died, rather than that person themselves. If we adopt this approach, we find that those who are in fact dying includes many who did not necessarily see themselves in this way, as we would expect, given the discussion above. Most importantly, it includes older people for whom dying is not something that is separable from an overall deterioration in physical health. Seale comments: 'People's status as "dying" is often only recognised when terminal illness is present... [but].... The care of the elderly *is* the care of the dying, just as it is also the care of the living' (Seale 1993). There is certainly a good case to be made for older people being considered as a second category of persons who are dying, with a key difference that this is likely to be unacknowledged in these terms.

Lastly, it is important to acknowledge that early death is likely for other groups of service users not often defined as 'dying'. People who are homeless or sleeping rough risk death through cold or neglect, and others through life-threatening behaviours such as drug abuse. These people too do not fit the picture of heroic victim which comes to mind when we speak of 'the dying'; their deaths are likely to be expected by others but not necessarily by themselves.

3.8 What is Dying?

Field (1996) suggests that the following features are characteristic of the modern dying role:

- entry is involuntary and directly linked to a medical definition that the illness is terminal;
- it is characterised by loss of activities and other roles, with little or no new activities;
- there is little prior socialisation into the role;
- there are no, or few, rites of passage to signal transition to the dying role;
- it is not a valued status.

Field argues that many of the most common causes of death – long-term chronic conditions – are not actually defined by medical practitioners as 'terminal' (1996: 263). There is no question here of deliberate deception, merely that chronic conditions, although known to lead to death, are not perceived in the same way as illnesses such as cancer. This has implications for their dying since they do not explicitly enter the 'dying role'. This is also the case for many older people who die in residential care.

We have already identified that death is both a bodily and a social event. For Seale, dying is severance of the social bond. 'Disruption of the social bond occurs as the body fails, self identity becomes harder to hold together and the normal expectations of human relations cannot be fulfilled' (1998: 149). Three levels can be seen in this analysis: firstly, that of the physical body ('as the body fails'); secondly, the level of self-identity; and thirdly, the social level of 'human relations'. In this analysis, the three are not really separable, since the body and social interaction are each part of what constitutes the ongoing project of self-identity. Since this analysis does not depend upon awareness of dying, it may be applied to each of the groups identified above. Clearly, the failure of the body is often primary, with self-identity and human relations dependent upon it, but there may be instances in which failure of the body results from the disintegration of social bonds or of self-identity, as in suicide or self-harm resulting in death.

To answer the question 'what is dying?' we can reply therefore that it involves aspects of physical deterioration or illness; an emotional or individual component concerning the self, and a social dimension which is about interaction with others. To these, some would add a spiritual dimension, but for others this might be considered to be part of the individual's self-reflection.

3.9   Facing Death: Psychological Perspectives

Theoretical understanding of dying has been dominated by work that considers the emotional state of individuals who are aware of their own coming death. This has tended to be from a psychological perspective, in which emotional states are seen as 'natural' and 'universal'. Walter (1994) and Seale (1998) see this focus upon the individual facing death as characteristic of the current period, in which psychology and patient-centred medicine are dominant 'discourses'. Such deaths are seen as 'heroic journeys' and institutional arrangements such as hospice care offer those who die in such circumstances the opportunity to 'live until they die'. Yet not all are eligible for such dying, as we have seen, and not all who are eligible accept the 'script' which is offered to them.

The work of the psychiatrist Elisabeth Kubler-Ross, first published in Britain in 1970, and now a classic, has been hugely influential, and formed a cornerstone for the psychological understanding of dying. She says in the preface to her book that 'it is not meant to be a textbook on how to manage dying patients, nor is it intended as a complete study of the psychology of the dying' (1970). Her work has come to be seen as both of these things. In the experiences of her dying patients, she identified five elements. These are:

- Denial
- Anger
- Bargaining
- Depression
- Acceptance

These have been identified as common reactions to terminal diagnosis, with a tendency for practitioners to try to help people to 'move on' from their initial denial towards acceptance. Since entry to this dying role is predicated upon awareness, denial (the first stage) is clearly a key issue. Sheldon (1997) spends some time elaborating the concept of denial, which may be seen either as a defence mechanism by those from a Freudian tradition, or as a coping mechanism. Either way, this is an unconscious process, identified as pathological in the first inter-pretation, and healthy in the second. She is at pains to distinguish denial from the conscious process of suppression of unwelcome news and from disagreement with a professional view, and later in the same chap-ter illustrates ways of working with people who are 'in denial' (Sheldon 1997: 62–4). The work of Kubler-Ross has become so well known that aspects of it have entered into lay people's own understandings, as we shall see in the next chapter.

Again, Seale offers us a contrast, pointing to an alternative 'script' of 'unaware dying'. This may take the form of active resistance by the patient, or sometimes be chosen by relatives who ask that the patient should not be informed of the diagnosis. It offers advantages in terms of the ability to continue life as normal, and care and emotional accom-paniment by relatives who may consciously take on the burden of 'knowing' on behalf of the person who is dying. From research evidence, there seem to be cultural differences in the choice of such 'scripts'. In Japan and Italy, for example, the principle of autonomy is less highly held that in Britain or America, and it is considered right for relatives to take control (Seale *et al.* 1997, and discussion in Seale 1998: 111–12). From the USA, a social worker (Smith 1993) describes an instance in which a patient and his wife insisted upon denying that he was close to death, on the basis of a firm shared religious conviction that he would be healed. Smith asks whether the social work practitioner – used to a role of helping people to acknowledge and accept 'the truth' – should challenge such insistence? As an apparently conscious decision on the part of the man concerned, this response is probably to be seen, not as denial, but as 'disagreement', in Sheldon's terms (1997: 62–4) or as 'suspended open awareness' (Timmermans 1994; see section 3.7). It does, however, illustrate the way in which strict adherence to any model can give rise to an ethical dilemma for the practitioner.

Two examples of service users in Britain who adopted their own, alternative 'scripts' which involved rejection of the acceptance of their own coming death, are given below. These are taken from my own interviews with social workers; in one instance the speaker was working in a specialist setting; in the other, a general one.

■ The social worker was asked by ward nurses to speak to a patient who was refusing to acknowledge that she was dying. 'I'm fed up with all this death and dying stuff', she said. 'Leave me alone.' The social worker argued that it was very important for staff to respect her wish not to discuss her death.

■ A seventy-year-old white man had been known for the past five years to have cancer of the prostate. His wife who cared for him at home was ten years his senior. He came into hospital 'off his legs', but wanted to return home. He had been very active, a vocal advocate for his daughter who had a learning disability. A smallish package of home care was arranged for after his discharge, which he later cancelled. Colleagues criticised the social worker for a bad discharge, but she insisted that it was not bad, only risky. He since got himself walking, and kept pushing the boundaries of what he had been told he could do. The social worker said that he knew exactly what was happening and chose to act as if it were not – this was uncomfortable for professionals because he did not conform to expected patterns for a dying person. The problem was theirs, not his.

These are both examples of people who have chosen not to conform, and who challenge professional expectations. It would be wrong, however, to give the impression that the reactions outlined by Kubler-Ross cannot be seen in the ways in which people adjust to awareness of their own death, or that it cannot be a useful tool for practitioners. In a culture where anger is an emotion that is often suppressed, for example, it can be particularly reassuring for people to be assured that this is an emotion that is common. The use that has been made of Kubler-Ross's work is a good example of the ways in which models and frameworks can be adopted in a rigid or prescriptive way, however.

Since the pioneering work of Kubler-Ross, Buckman has put forward an 'alternative framework...which more accurately reflects the dying patient's progress and will allow the professional greater power of analysis and prediction' (Buckman 1998: 146). This model is as follows:

- *Initial stage – 'facing the threat'*
  A mixture of reactions which are characteristic of the individual and may include any, or all, of the following:
  Fear, anxiety, shock, disbelief, anger, denial, guilt, humour, hope/despair, bargaining.
- *Chronic stage – 'being ill'*
  1. Resolution of those elements of the initial response which are resolvable.
  2. Diminution of intensity of all emotions – 'monochrome state'.
  3. Depression is very common.

- *Final stage – acceptance*
  1. Defined by the patient's acceptance of death.
  2. Not an essential state provided that the patient is not distressed, is communicating normally, and is making decisions normally.

The two service users who were referred to above would probably be no happier with Buckman's model than with that of Kubler-Ross, for it was precisely the professional's 'power of analysis and prediction' against which they were protesting. There is an inherent dilemma here for the worker. At times, empowering the service user means defending their right to reject both the help offered and the models on which it is based.

Buckman's model is, like that of Kubler-Ross, essentially about the emotional reactions of the dying person. Corr (1992) reminds us that the dying person has other needs. He offers a descriptive model of four 'tasks' for dying people:

- To satisfy bodily needs and minimise physical distress in ways that are consistent with other values.
- To maximise psychological security, autonomy and richness in living.
- To sustain and enhance those interpersonal attachments significant to the dying person and to address the social implications of dying.
- To identify, develop or reaffirm sources of spiritual energy and in so doing foster hope.

This takes us back to a focus that is broader than the individual and his or her emotions, which is welcome. It runs the risk of being so broad that it is of little help, except perhaps as a checklist. The third 'task' is one of particular importance for the social carer, however, and is as applicable to people who are reaching the end of their life as a consequence of advanced age as to those who have a terminal illness. For one specialist social worker, 'helping to resolve unfinished business', usually of a social nature, is a particular aspect of her work with people who are aware they are dying. In a parallel way, many older people who have no terminal diagnosis spend time 'putting their affairs in order' whilst they are still able to do so; perhaps distributing particular sentimental items between family members in advance of their death.

In the previous sections, I have considered not only some of the theoretical understandings concerning the emotional responses of people who come to know that they are dying, but also asked questions about how this term is used and which groups of people can be considered to be dying. This helps us to answer questions concerning the extent of involvement that social care workers have with dying people. Clearly, there are practitioners who are part of specialist palliative care services which are specifically designed to offer care and advice to dying people, both adults and children. Part of the role of these services is to offer consultancy and advice to others who work with those who are dying. Increasingly, it is being recognised that this needs to include those who provide care for older people either in their own homes or in institutional settings (Di Mola 1997; Siddell, Katz and Komaromy 1998).

To be effective, consultancy or advice from specialists needs to be offered by those who have some awareness of the constraints and pressures facing generalist workers. Given the rate of change in statutory social care, it is hard even for those within the services to keep abreast of developments. One specialist hospice social worker describes liaison with colleagues in statutory services as an essential aspect of her role. This liaison is based upon shared professional identity and a sympathetic approach to the current constraints and changes in mainstream social care. There is evidence that GPs and district nurses may not always welcome the advice of medical or nursing palliative care experts (Sidell, Katz and Komaromy 1998), or may feel undermined by it. It can, of course, be an enormous advantage for specialists in palliative care to work in informed partnership with generalists in the community. To do so effectively at the levels of policy and of practice seems to require mutual respect for each other's role. A common professional background is one factor that can facilitate this.

As well as consultancy from experts in palliative care, whether themselves social workers or not, social carers working with people who are dying need their own understanding and awareness of key issues. In addition to the concepts introduced here, this is likely to include some knowledge of what to expect in practical terms, of what dying people most fear and of how to enable them to discuss their death should they wish to do so. Another area in which training may be helpful is in relation to systems for managing the feelings and fears of staff members. In specialist settings where dying is an explicit feature of the work, good practice has developed. In generalist settings, workers are familiar with the issues and dilemmas, but may be less confident in working with them.

4

Facing Death

Having outlined some of the ways in which dying has been understood 'from the outside' or by those not in this situation themselves, the aim of this chapter is to let some people who are dying describe their experience in their own words, as far as possible. It should not be surprising that amongst those who write about their experience of facing death there are those who are writers by profession – journalists or novelists. I draw here on the books by Oscar Moore, who died aged 36 years in 1996 following nearly three years with AIDS (Moore 1996), and of Ruth Picardie, who died of cancer in 1997, aged 33 years (Picardie 1998). Both were journalists and both wrote of their experiences in a national newspaper column; their last column being, in each case, about a month before they died. I also refer to a newspaper article (Brodkey 1996) by the American novelist Harold Brodkey, who died in 1996, also as a result of AIDS.

In order to broaden the 'pool' of experiences, I have selected as well from some research accounts that are heavily based upon first-hand experience. The first are two reports commissioned by Norfolk Social Services Department (Davies 1995 and Frankham 1996) to investigate and document the experiences of those in that area who were HIV positive or had AIDS. The second is the book by Young and Cullen (1996) whose subtitle is 'conversations with East Londoners'. This reports the experience of 14 people with cancer during their last year of life. These research accounts take us a little further from the direct accounts of dying people, but they have the advantage that they can, by this very token, give us an insight into the experience of those who do not choose to write their own story. They include the experiences therefore of those who are less socially confident or articulate, and some who have fewer resources (whether of money or in terms of social support). In the case of Young and Cullen's work, they include some older people (half are over 70 years, and the oldest is 94 years).

Even with these additions, however, the bias of my sources is evident. Cancer and AIDS are not numerically the most prevalent causes of death, as already discussed. Nonetheless, they are the causes most characteristic of the 'aware dying role' that was explored in the last chapter. It is important to note that missing here are, amongst others, the views of older people without cancer, of children or adolescents with life-threatening disease, of those who have a learning disability and the experiences of those in residential rather than community settings. The accounts included here are not therefore cited as representative. Their purpose is to stimulate that creative imagination that will enable readers to hear as unique every account, whether written or in their own practice, and also to provide some commentary upon theoretical understandings. This will give us a good platform from which to look at the experience of social care practitioners who work with people facing death, and to consider their responses – the subjects of the chapter that follows this.

Three themes have been apparent within these accounts, representing key aspects of the experiences described. The second – abandoning the future – is the aspect of dying that dominates theoretical accounts. The first and third – managing the present, and issues to do with relating to others – are of particular interest and importance to social care workers.

4.1　Managing the Present

'Dying is strenuous work which demands new skills and new outlooks if independence is to be preserved.' 'When dying people are least adaptable they are called on to be more so. No healthy person has to make such sharp adjustments in such short order' (Young and Cullen 1996: 61 and 63). For most people for whom dying is a slow business, the process is not just a psychological one of mental adjustment. As people whose bodily health is failing, there is a lot to do in the present. Much of this is directly connected to the illness itself. There are two main aspects to this: the illness itself, and the implications of it – such as treatment routines.

In terms of the illness itself, Oscar Moore speaks for many in saying that 'I live by the uneven rhythm of my guts' (1996: xxiii). Although there are clearly differences between illnesses in terms of their particular physical implications, bodily changes come to dominate life and what is possible. Then there are the implications of seeking and receiving treatment. Five months before her death, Ruth Picardie wrote that 'my whole life seems to have been taken over by illness' (1998: 30), going on to give examples of appointments that occupied her time.

Later, she speaks of coming to terms with her prognosis, but also of 'all the stuff I've got to do now', and comments that 'it's bloody tough living in limbo, not knowing exactly how long I've got left. Do I get a four-month or a twelve-month prescription prepayment certificate?' (p. 58). Oscar Moore's book is dominated (in terms of words, if not its overall message) by accounts of his declining physical condition, and of periods of immobility or hospitalisation. A Londoner himself, living in easy walking distance of major hospitals, he acknowledges, moreover, the increased inconvenience and time issues for those living outside London, citing a correspondent who 'has to travel fifty miles for a routine consultation' (1996: 147). For the people in Young and Cullen's (1996) study, there are daily routines created to manage the pills to be taken, and to manage life generally. These routines impose order and routine in situations that are in many ways outside the individual's control. Illness and treatment therefore become dominant, and are very time-consuming.

Some comment that this obscures the distinction between body and mind. Thus, Oscar Moore writes of the way that 'my life was about to implode and that curious determination to keep the mind and body in self contained airtight compartments was about to be made to look ridiculous' (1996: xxxii). Brodkey (1996) says 'now one belongs entirely to nature, to time; identity was a game'. Young and Cullen also report a disturbance of the body–mind relation, suggesting that 'instead of being one body, they were two, a body which was afflicted and a mind looking on' (1996: 39) saying that 'their bodies were no longer the silent, uncomplaining companions they had once been. Their bodies had turned traitor' (p. 9). They go on to speak of the constraints of illness as follows: 'they were surrounded by a whole new set of constraints, generally much tighter than those they had displaced. From the time that the illness took hold, and increasingly as it bit deeper, their lives were under the domination of inescapables, of external forces that were beyond their control' (p. 9).

Other external matters occupy the present. Housing was an issue for all included in the first Norfolk report (Davies 1995), and all had moved at least once since diagnosis. The social worker comments, 'people seem to find themselves in private upstairs flats that aren't going to be suitable when they become unwell, or that are too small to have a carer living in. We've had people coming out of mobile homes, travellers . . . who've needed accommodation, people that have become homeless through debt; all sorts needing homes' (Davies 1995: 17). There may need to be adaptation of living accommodation where someone is to die at home: for example, 'the family worked on Peter's house to make it more suitable for him. He lived on the top floor because there was no downstairs toilet and bathroom to which he might need immediate access' (p. 52). In Young and Cullen's study, we find that 'as people's range was further cut down, they could not manage stairs and were confined to the span of a room or two on one level' (1996: 41). Within such living space, aspects of living that used to be commonplace become a major enterprise. A carer, Ivy, in Young and Cullen's study says, for example, 'we managed a bath this week. Each time it's a little more difficult' (p. 42). Financial issues arise. Oscar Moore: 'I have entered benefit land' (1996: 60). Ruth Picardie describes her assessment for subsidised cleaning (1998: 42–3). For those with fewer personal resources, financial constraints and concerns may determine other possibilities of daily life. Such practicalities are, of course, the daily work of social care.

Managing the present is clearly both a practical and an emotional matter. It involves being dominated by bodily functions, routines and treatments, and establishing ways of coping with diminishing abilities without losing more control or independence than is necessary. Body, mind and social relations are all part of managing the present. As we have seen, the body increasingly dominates this threesome. Dependence upon others also increases, but it is clear in those accounts I have read that a mental process is also involved. Oscar Moore moves from 'I have not felt as if I am in control of what is going on for as long as these problems have been active' to comment two paragraphs later in the same letter that now he is feeling better 'all is not lost. I am having a good time' (1996: xxviii–xxix). He describes work and leisure, and the need to 'live each day carefully because there may not be enough left to go round' (p. xix). As the pain and physical symptoms of this episode pass, control of the present is re-established. AIDS is characterised by recurrent serious bouts of illness, unlike cancer, where control, once relinquished, is hard to regain, although even here there may be short periods of remission. After a period of decline and hospitalisation right at the end of her life, Ruth Picardie recovered sufficiently to enjoy a party in the park with her family.

The social aspect of managing the present lies for most people in the threat posed by willing helpers to dignity and to independence. I consider this aspect below with other matters relating to changed relationships with others. For some people with AIDS, however, there is a much more sinister threat from other people. Some of the respondents in Norfolk spoke of threats, attack and hostility. Thus Jim says 'I have been stopped in the street by someone saying "I hear you're HIV posit-ive". I've had people threatening to break my legs; gay community guys, people I don't know particularly well. . . . All sorts of crazy things gener-ated through fear' (Jim, in Davies 1995: 26). Another man had had his flat attacked 13 times. These experiences do not fit well with our pre-conceptions about dying; they seem to belong to an earlier era, when fear led to dying people being abandoned or ostracised. Most journal-istic accounts are written by people who live amongst people anxious to help; fear of suffocation by kindness a greater threat than fear of attack. Yet clearly managing the present may, for some, involve less socially acceptable struggles.

The present then is precarious. Difficult balances must be struck – for most between losing control either to others who seek to help or to the body that threatens to overwhelm. These balances are perhaps more difficult for those who wish to retain independence; some people give in more easily either to the bodily processes or to the ministrations of others. Even so, the present has to be endured and managed, and it seems to be the case in all the accounts I have looked at that this is likely to involve many new tasks, challenges and occupations. I turn next to look at the aspect of dying that comes most readily to mind when we speak of dying: abandoning the future.

4.2 Abandoning the Future

'What hurts most is losing the future', writes Ruth Picardie. 'The future will get on just fine without me . . . It's just that I'll miss it so' (1998: 58–9). 'I can't say, "*I will see you this summer*" . . . Memory . . . has to be ended, has to be put aside, as if one were leaving a chapel and bringing the prayer to an end in one's head' (Brodkey 1996). 'I shan't be a bit sorry to die, to see if there is an afterlife or if there is not one, so it is a great adventure' (Harold Allen, 75 years, from Young and Cullen 1996: 22). 'I really do wish I was dead. I can see no future now. I just keep pegging on 'til I peg it now' (Dean, 23-years-old, cited in Davies 1995: 28). These very differ-ent quotes all reflect awareness that there will be no future; the speakers differ in their attitude toward that realisation, usually depending upon their view of what that future might have held. For Dean, this was not a lot, for Ruth it was a great deal. What is involved in coming to this real-isation that there is little or no future, at least in this life?

It is in looking at people's accounts of the process of realisation of their own dying that we come closest to the responses as described by

Kubler-Ross (1970; and above, section 3.9). It is also clear that these have become part of the way some people themselves look at their own reactions. The idea of being 'in denial', for example, has become to some extent a lay concept – 'by the way, is it just me, or is everyone in denial these days and where were they before?' asks Moore in a characteristic aside (1996: 4). Awareness is, as most commentators now stress, not a 'once for all' process, nor one that proceeds in an orderly fashion. Let us look at the progression in one account. Ruth Picardie writes on 20 November 1996 concerning treatment for cancer at the start of her illness that it 'makes you look sick, feel you are dying, which I am not' (1998: 1). To the same friend, she writes on 10 April 1997, 'I still can't quite believe I am going to die and, deep down, assume that there will be some miracle' (p. 31). To another friend, a month later (8 May 1997), she writes '... have been told I only have a few months to live... Definitely time to find a new godmother' (p. 33). In June, '... might have a year's remission: if not, it'll be curtains this year, which I really can't believe since I am not in pain/losing weight etc. Hence no blowing of savings on round the world trip since I think I'm in denial' (p. 35). Later that month (22 June 1997), she writes about this process of realisation in *The Observer* Life. Initially, she says, 'the Clooney-luvin' Pollyanna inside you just won't give in'. Then, some months later, as the news of the condition's spread worsens, 'you enter the bleakly euphemistic world of palliative care. Pollyanna commits suicide' (p. 39). Less than two months later, her column of 3 August contains the words 'the bottom line is, I'm dying' (p. 57). This period is filled with e-mails to friends that reflect this process of physical deterioration and mental realisation. About a fortnight before she dies (12 September 1997), she writes 'I feel close to the end now – weary and in pain' (Picardie 1998: 90).

All the emotions and reactions described by theorists are there in Ruth Picardie's writing alongside her humour: anger (p. 38) and feeling 'so grumpy and depressed' (p. 39). 'I veer between weeping, feeling totally emotionally and physically drained and being unable to believe I am going to die this year' (p. 53), she writes even after the diagnosis of her brain tumour. There is bargaining too in her pursuit of alternative and complementary therapies. 'You desperately want to lengthen the odds', she says of her previous preoccupation with such therapies – 'the panic and desperate hope of a girl with cancer knows no bounds... I have now come to my senses' (p. 77; 17 August 1997). Both complementary and mainstream treatments have failed. This progression is apparent, too, in Oscar Moore's account. Thus, of the time when his HIV-positive status became AIDS, he writes 'I didn't feel ready for a change' and 'it has been a long journey out of denial' (1996: 4). Later, he also speaks of seeking remedies in much the same way as Ruth Picardie was to do: 'desperate men seek desperate remedies' (p. 10).

For Oscar Moore, however, there is a temporary change as new drug treatments bring real benefits and hope. He describes the reversal thus: 'In 1994, I acclimatised myself to a premature death. . . . I took comfort in small pleasures and narrow horizons . . . but as 1995 starts in a flurry of breakthroughs, I am banking on life not life insurance' (1996: 75). Yet the loss is continuing despite this. He continues, 'But nothing is certain. The light at the end of the tunnel keeps going out of focus. . . . Already a crucial battle has been lost: I have relinquished my car. . . . Driving a car had come to seem inextricably intertwined with my independence as a citizen, my status as an adult and my potency as a man' (p. 76). The process of realisation and of abandoning the future is therefore more like a switchback than a straightforward journey, not least due to real changes of prognosis in some instances.

The question of whether to fight or to give in is present in a number of accounts. Oscar Moore asks: 'Is suicide laziness, cowardice, cynicism or rebellion?' (1996: xxviii). Tony (in Davies 1995) asks directly 'Who's got it right? Are the people who said "I can't handle this, I don't want to handle this" or "I'm chicken" . . . so they give themselves permission very early . . . Or have I got it right by fighting? I can't fight and beat it, I'm not that much of a fool. But am I fighting just to have yet another painful episode? . . . Who's got it right?' (Tony, in Davies, p. 47). Tony also speaks of the way that life is reducing. 'Life becomes very much smaller against your wishes and against your will. You are constantly fighting against the fact that you have got to ask for help.' 'You have to admit a lot, you have to accept more and more limitations which is a damage to your pride. You have to accept that you survive at decreasing levels of efficiency and you realise every few months "Well, I'll never be that again"' (Tony, in Davies, p. 46). There are echoes here of Oscar Moore: 'so I retired, adding dancing to the growing list of things we used to do when we were young . . . or at least fit and well' (1996: 117).

For some, hope and optimism in face of such catalogues of loss are essential to continued survival. 'Optimism has become my most important drug . . . low spirits lead to low resistance' (Moore 1996: 59). He later writes: 'a large part of this war is psychological; just as stress is a pernicious helpmate to the onset of illness, so optimism is a crucial part of the defence. Mind and body are not separate' (p. 129). Ruth Picardie agrees. 'You can't give up hope because (a) people who believe they are going to die, die sooner and (b) living without hope is miserable' (1998: 44). This observation may seem strangely placed in a section about abandoning the future. This hope has a different quality, however, to the desperate bargaining of seeking miracle cures. It is not necessarily hope for longer life, but part of a hopeful or optimistic attitude that coexists with the acceptance of dying.

So, too, people also paradoxically speak of a changed relationship to time, and a greater connectedness to life. Oscar Moore again: 'It makes me look at the world more keenly and yet sometimes I feel as if I am looking at it through someone else's window' (1996: xxix). 'Suddenly I seem to understand the infinite stretch of the space-time continuum and how there will always be time to do the things that matter and how everything else can wait' (p. 48), though he does put this down to a side-effect of the drugs. Ruth Picardie is sceptical of the idea that terminal illness has made her wise, insisting instead that the diagnosis 'turns you into a grumpy, bitter, envious cow' (1998: 38), but she writes with enthusiasm of her 'retail therapy' which consists of 'personal indulgence or escapism of any kind' (p. 78). Barry (in Davies 1995) says 'I know that in the past six months I've changed in quite profound ways. Beforehand, you'd get very uptight about a lot of things, like you have to prove things in life, I suppose. Waiting to have enough for when you retire. But you begin to look at things in context, and you start to live for the day. That does change you' (Barry, in Davies, pp. 9–10). 'Since I've known, I've actually controlled my life more than any time and it's been extremely positive. This was mirrored by a friend of mine who's got AIDS and he said it was one of the best things that actually happened to his life because it empowered him to take control of things. There he was being ill and he was off to Hong Kong the next week for a holiday and is doing an MA in something or other, because you're living that bit more' (Barry, in Davies, p. 10). Again, Oscar Moore agrees, saying 'At times, I feel that I am, for the first time, in full possession of my life ...'. Realism is part of this, though. He continues 'Then, of course, something goes wrong and I am rudely reminded that I am no longer running my own body', but concludes that for the moment 'I'm putting panic on hold and concentrating on the immediate' (1996: 64). Jim's reaction to the awareness of a shortened time is a contrast to this. He says, 'things become very urgent, so I suddenly become very, very intolerant of inefficiency. I will not wait for anything. I just see my life trickling away' (Jim, in Davies 1995: 11). Harold Brodkey acknowledges the lack of a future, saying, 'To the end of the century, I said when I was asked [how long he wanted to live]. Well, I won't make it.' Time seems for him collapsed; there is a strong sense of continuity with the past as well as this same focus upon the present moment, the now: 'I am sensible of the velocity of the moments ... I hear each moment whisper as it slides along. And yet I am very happy ...' (Brodkey 1996).

What then can we say about the process of abandoning the future? It is observable in these accounts. It is not a straightforward or linear process. It involves the emotions many have described. It is not entirely negative. It seems to entail a series of revisions of a person's worldview and their relation to the present and to the past. It contains too, an element of optimism in some instances, which does not seem incompatible with an overall acceptance of the inevitability of death. Yet we cannot and should not sanitise it. Not all the accounts are of those who accepted the prognosis. A number resisted or denied it to the end. This was so of three of the fourteen studied by Young and Cullen, and for one of the young men in the Norfolk study. And as Ruth Picardie's partner Matt writes, 'dying is nasty, ugly and painful' in many instances. He describes Ruth's attitude as 'a way of *both* defying *and* accepting her cancer' (my emphasis), as well as 'a piece of performance for our benefit. ... Before she became too ill to care, Ruth was hilariously impatient with people she felt were inadequate in dealing with the fact that she had cancer' (Picardie 1998: 100). It is to this that we turn next; the issue of dying as separation and how those who are themselves facing death perceive others.

4.3 Separation, Loneliness and the Social Bond

'But with a progressive disease like cancer, dying is a relentlessly attritional process of estrangement. You want so much to do and say the right thing, but you are doomed to frustration, failure and regret.' '... in retrospect, the lump not only grew within her, but between us. ... I often felt that, as Ruth was dying, our relationship was by degrees dying with her.' 'The dying person has to break her bonds with the world, to separate herself off: it is the process of alienation I still bitterly regret, but it is also a necessary part of letting go.' 'I knew then that the true meaning of dying is its absolute loneliness' (Matt Seaton, in Picardie 1998: 103, 114, 115). These are the observations of one who was centrally involved in caring for Ruth as she died. To what extent do they reflect the view of those themselves facing death? The theme of connectedness and loneliness does indeed run through these accounts. We can identify several kinds of connection or estrangement: to or

from 'others' generally, especially those not dying; to or from acquaintances, and to or from those who are close. There is also the company of
'fellow travellers' – others who are dying, who may or may not be
personally known.

Oscar Moore describes being sick as 'to find myself left alone and
increasingly left out. I was outside the perimeter fence staring through
the chain link of my sick room window as life went on the other/outside'
(1996: 17). 'I feel left out, left behind, marginalised' (p. xxix). About sex
and 'the chase', he writes 'it's the best game in town, and I feel disquali-
fied' (p. 25). In a piece about company, we find the comment that 'the
loneliness of illness is one of its bitterest aspects – especially as every
day on the streets rudely healthy people seem to push us out of the way'
(p. 63). Dean has the same condition as Moore, but lacks close friendships, and has suffered attack and abuse. He says of others in general,
'I just feel outcast, still, still feel outcast now – its horrid' (Dean, in
Davies 1995: 21).

Regarding others who are known, but not close friends, the attitudes
of some acquaintances have been a 'considerable source of anger and
disgust' to Toni and Joe. 'People didn't seem to care when Joe was so
ill, and have looked the other way when Joe is in the wheelchair', leading his partner to comment 'I'd rather be lonely than put up with that
crap' (Frankham 1996: 15). Speakers differ in relation to their wish for
general sympathy. Paul is not gay, but is HIV-positive – something that
has made him feel different and cut off: 'unless you're standing up
saying I'm gay or I'm bisexual, or I'm this or I'm that, nobody wants to
know' (Paul, in Frankham 1996: 36). He is clear that 'I wouldn't want
sympathy myself. It's just my way of getting through it.... When I'm
unwell I lock the door and I don't let anybody in' (p. 39). Ruth Picardie's
friend Jamie agrees: 'The main reason I keep my stuff strictly limited
publicity wise is I couldn't face dealing with sorrow, grief, whingeing,
sympathy, worry and shit. Other people's reactions in other words'
(Jamie, in Picardie 1998: 8). She challenges this in her reply: 'I don't
know how you have survived without telling the whole world and his
aunt about your status – don't you want sympathy, empathy, chocs?
I know there's shit involved, too...e.g. endless phone calls demanding
detailed analysis of your emotional and physiological state'(p. 12). She
later writes in *The Observer* about her increased popularity since becoming ill: 'people I haven't seen for years wanting to take me out to lunch
...why all this interest in sick people?' Some, she suggests 'reckon that
cripples can help them get to heaven'. Others 'seem to find terminal
illness exciting, the secular Samaritans looking for glory' (p. 73).

Different again are the responses of close friends, which may be a source of comfort. Following an afternoon and evening with six friends, Oscar Moore says 'the sheer warmth of human contact, the laughter and chatter, the reminiscences and the gossiping, had left me invigorated. ... as my long-term ambitions hit short-term realities, and thoughts of the future became at best redundant and at worst panic-stricken, it is these evenings and these people ... which have provided the meaning in my life' (Moore 1996: 62). He also comments on the comfort of letters from strangers, and growing friendships with professional carers, so this is not just about proximity. Clearly, for some people, close friends vary greatly in whether they 'get it right'. Ruth Picardie comments at various times as follows. 'He [husband Matt] is being amazingly unsupportive and egocentric.... I guess he doesn't have anything left over at the moment' (1998: 3). 'Justine [sister] continues to be amazingly supportive and helpful' (p. 9). 'Matt is being stoical, though God knows how much fear and misery he is repressing' (p. 14). 'Dearest, bestest Carrie, Thank you for your wonderful e-mail, which said all the right things' (p. 53). Joe (in Frankham 1996) rejects all concern, even from close family. He speaks of his resentment at the changes his illness causes in the behaviour, not just of those who don't want to know, but of those who are concerned to help. 'Unfortunately, my picture of it is cotton wool. Pampered. Followed round. Watched over. Like I'm an old biddy in an old biddy's home ... I don't want that' (Joe, in Frankham, p. 12). He allows his partner in, however, and also, in time, the social worker.

There are comments about the different quality of relationships with those who are similarly placed. 'It feels good to have a friend who is sick too', writes Ruth to a friend who is HIV positive; 'there's a level of connection that even the most supportive friends can't achieve' (Picardie 1998: 6). This is the 'secret fraternity of sickness between people ... whose tales of hell and high water in the pursuit of temporary relief from terminal crises provide a mutual support. Somehow the reflection of one's own miseries in someone else's life soothes the pain of suffering' (Moore 1996: 62–3). Yet not all fellow sufferers provide such comfort. Ruth speaks of the distance between herself and 'the sad, bald fucks you meet in hospital the whole time' (Picardie 1998: 6).

In a situation of increasing dependence on others that may be welcomed or bitterly resented, terminal illness both highlights the characteristics of existing relationships (including, for some people, a lack of close attachments) and creates its own new struggles. These struggles are typically around these very issues of dependence and dignity. There is heightened sensitivity on both sides. As we shall see, this is also characteristic of bereavement, underlining that facing one's own death involves grief, as much as living after the death of another. Yet the dangers of 'getting it wrong' do not constitute sufficient reason for leaving the dying person alone. As one carer said of his partner's father, from whom both had suffered considerable hostility, 'you can forgive him everything because at least he was there' (Tony, in Davies 1996: 45).

4.4 Some Reflections upon Theory

Whilst the individuality of the experience of dying is apparent from these extracts, so too some patterns emerge. The nature of the illness (and hence of the dying process), the age of the person who is dying, their gender, the extent of their social networks, their financial and physical resources; their personality – these and other factors are clearly important. All these are factors identified also as determinants of grieving in bereavement, as we shall see in later chapters (Parkes 1996; Worden 1991; and below, section 6.2.1). Whilst acknowledging that this account is insufficient basis for a detailed critique of theoretical understandings, it is worth making a few observations on the theoretical understandings and models outlined in Chapter 3 in order to illustrate how the concepts can be applied.

The two main accounts – by Ruth Picardie and Oscar Moore – illustrate diseases with different dying trajectories. They show the importance of predictability – 'it's bloody tough, living in limbo, not knowing how long I've got left' (Picardie 1998: 58) – and also the fluctuation and uncertainty that is characteristic of AIDS (in Moore's accounts). Awareness contexts are also of relevance. By definition, those who write about their dying are those who are aware of it and willing to communicate this awareness, and the same is true of those who speak of their experiences to researchers. There is support, however, for Timmermans' elaboration of the open awareness category (1994). The issue of retaining hope (a feature of his 'uncertain open awareness') is there in Ruth Picardie's writings.

For most of the writers whose work is included here, social death can be seen as extending after biological death, rather than occurring before it, at least in the sense that their writing (and work like this that reviews it) is extending their influence and participation in social life. Yet Ruth Picardie's partner does describe a form of social death in speaking of the dying of their relationship. This also shows how social death can be true for some involved, but not all, since her relationship with her mother, sister and some friends seems to differ in this respect (although we do not have their accounts). The Norfolk accounts show some evidence of a process of social exclusion for some of those concerned, although not all.

These personal accounts illustrate well Seale's analysis of dying as severance of the social bond – 'as the body fails, self identity becomes harder to hold together and the normal expectations of human relations cannot be fulfilled' (1998: 149) – as discussed in the previous chapter. We can see all three strands in managing the present (where the failing body poses a particular threat), abandoning the future (in which issues of identity are central) and questions around the loneliness of dying.

Tensions and ambiguities are present in each area, however. The first strand – the body – does not always fail in a smooth way. There may be remissions; the implications of failure can be offset to some extent in some circumstances – or fought in others. Self-identity (the second and pivotal strand) is, as Seale and Giddens argue, an ongoing issue. In some ways it seems that identity may become, for some people, clearer or more transparent in dying, rather than harder to hold together. As Matt Seaton comments about Ruth: 'it was a very Ruth thing to do to write about her cancer in the way she did' (Picardie 1998: 97). Her book is not about a disintegrating identity but a triumphant one. One may argue that this is the whole purpose of a book that was put together and published by others after her death. What more obvious way to continue the project of reflexivity and creation of identity? This is in line with Tony Walter's identification of 'bereavement as biography' (1996) – a thesis whose roots lie in the same theoretical tradition as Seale's own work. This is discussed in more detail in Chapter 6, below, and relates to the issue of social death, as already acknowledged.

Yet one of the main conclusions of Young and Cullen's study is also about the importance of 'the spirit' for people in the process of dying. They write: 'what stands out is the significance of people's spirit – this for want of a better word for a quality that belongs to the whole personality and the whole reaction of that person to adversity' (Young and Cullen 1996: 36). 'The spirit did not need to weaken as the body weakened but could even get stronger. The spirit was something to hold on to, to be held up by and to be stubbornly proud of. The spirit was relatively timeless – the continuo above which the solemn and the gay were played out' (p. 62). They are commenting here on the accounts of people from the East End of London; many elderly, without fame or fortune. This quality that they identify in cancer patients in London is also apparent in the Norfolk studies reporting the experiences of people (predominantly gay young men) with AIDS. None of these people are publicly known in the way that Oscar Moore and Ruth Picardie were through their ability to be articulate and witty about their own dying. Self-identity, then, is not necessarily destroyed through dying – or even necessarily harder to hold together, although it does seem to be challenged and changed by it, as we saw in the accounts in section 4.2.

What can we say of human relationships, Seale's third strand? Again, there is some strengthening as well as increased distance apparent in the accounts. There are tensions, particularly in relation to issues of dependence, but some social relations continue to be important. In many ways it is clearly true that severance of the social bond is ultimately 'a necessary part of letting go', as Matt Seaton suggests. Perhaps a crucial factor here is the extent to which mental ability is retained intact, a point that very directly relates to the issue of social death, and also again reflects the fact that these are mainly accounts of people who are fully participating in social life until their death. Those caring for a relative with dementia, such as the respondents in the study by Sweeting and Gilhooly (1997), would no doubt give very different accounts of the issue of social relationships at the end of life.

Corr's (1992) four tasks (see Chapter 3, section 3.9) are, not surprisingly, apparent in these accounts. We can see issues to do with bodily needs feature largely in managing the present. Psychological security is an issue at the heart of the process of abandoning the future and adjustment to the fact of dying. Interpersonal attachments and social implications were discussed in section 4.3, and issues of spiritual energy have been highlighted above. The accounts do, for me, point to a complexity and level of struggle around these questions that is easily oversimplified in such a framework, however.

Buckman's model (1998) seems to share the problems of all 'stage theories': personal accounts of those who are dying both illustrate a progression and belie it. 'Facing the threat' of a terminal diagnosis seems to be an ongoing business, as does 'being ill'. Both acceptance and denial were to be found in these accounts at many stages as the illness progressed, and as the reality that the individual needed to accept altered. Some never reached acceptance, and did not wish to do so (as Buckman acknowledges); others seemed to reach small plateaux of acceptance at one level, but not at others. Ruth Picardie, for example, could write of being close to the end, whilst battling with her carers for independence almost to the last. Young and Cullen (1996) reflect upon

Kubler-Ross's sequences in the light of their data, concluding that 'since individual variation is so great, it is unlikely that any one conceptual system could be applied to all' (Young and Cullen 1996: 16). Yet they do identify a variety of issues that are likely to occupy the dying person and document variations around particular themes, which is helpful for practitioners. In a more limited way, this is what I have tried to do here. The reader is urged to supplement this through their own experience and reading, which will add richness and depth – and sometimes challenge – to theoretical understandings.

5

Care Workers' Involvement with Those Facing Their Own Death

The last chapter considered the experience of people who are facing death. Here, I look at the experience of social care practitioners whose work brings them into contact with them. The first section of this chapter offers examples, from across the range of social care services, of situations in which the anticipated or imminent death of the service user is a significant factor in the work to be done. The section that follows relates to the workers' responses. What is the role of the practitioner? What is distinctive about it, and what are some of the practice issues and tensions? Links will be made with the features identified in Chapter 2 as characteristic of social care (section 2.3). The last section identifies specialist skills and knowledge that are seen by the workers involved to underpin their current work with dying people, and the training and support that is available to them. Throughout the chapter, use will be made, as appropriate, of the theoretical concepts identified in Chapter 3, and references made to the experiences and needs of dying people, as discussed in Chapter 4.

In claiming that work with people who are facing death is a feature of many settings, I am not, of course, arguing that the frequency of such contact is identical in all. Although examples are deliberately drawn from a broad spectrum of services, those who work in palliative care or in specialist services (where this fact is the focus for involvement) have developed expertise in this area and have much to teach those workers for whom such involvement is infrequent. In settings where work with dying people is infrequent, there are, however, other overriding priorities and imperatives that cannot be put aside, and these must be understood by any who seek to extend the scope or nature of work to be done. Social care workers in settings where dying is not a frequent occurrence have their own expertise. With understanding of some main issues and principles, they can – and, in many cases, already do – respond appropriately to the situation of those facing their own death, as the need arises in the context of their other work.

5.1 Social Care with People Facing Death: A Broad Spectrum

Three categories are used in this section: death in childhood; untimely adult deaths; and death and dying as encountered by those working in services for older people – technically those over 65 years, but increasingly a more aged group. Any categorisation has drawbacks, but this is chosen deliberately to reflect both aspects of theory and of practice. Separate consideration of death and dying in childhood reflects legislative and service boundaries, but also reminds us that the experience of children does differ both in terms of their level of understanding, and their frequent lack of power or control over their own lives. In relation to children close to death, much of the work done is to support their parents or other primary carers.

The division between deaths amongst older people and those in adulthood which are seen as 'untimely' is one that reflects practice divisions and the arrangement of services, but which warrants some discussion. There is the fact, already discussed (section 3.7) that, excepting those with cancer, older people are rarely admitted to the 'aware dying role'. Services for older people are usually not acknowledged to be services for those who are dying. Hospice and palliative care services are mainly for those who have cancer, and are therefore more heavily weighted towards those who die at an earlier age, although not excluding older people. It is also younger people who have contributed most to writing about their own experiences, looked at in the last chapter. Yet an age-based distinction is in part an artificial one: many deaths of individuals aged over 65 years may well be considered 'untimely'. Might not a distinction based upon diagnosis have more reality for a service user?

Age does (in a general sense) correspond, however, both to some social considerations (the likelihood of having dependent children or being in paid employment, for example) and to a lay sense of a 'natural order' in which those who are older are expected to predecease their children. Moreover, we find that within the literature concerning dying, from a medical perspective, the deaths of 'elderly people' tend to be separated from those relating to particular diagnostic categories (e.g. Victor 1993; George and Sykes 1997). George and Sykes (1997) review a number of factors that justify this distinction, which include the presence, in elderly people, of multiple diagnoses, difficulty in defining dying until close to death, increased likelihood of communication problems and the likelihood of reduced social networks. The relation of such factors with a specific cut-off point in terms of age is clearly very imprecise in particular cases. In general terms, however, a distinction of this kind has been found useful for those planning services.

Further, it is the case that a grouping that does not follow the medical model of diagnoses can alert us to other categories of persons who are dying. We have seen how, in Britain, the term 'dying' is currently likely to be reserved for those with a particular disease that is seen to be terminal, and that the medical profession are thus now the gatekeepers to the 'aware dying role' (Seale 1998). In global terms, however, dying has another face. Destitution, poverty and starvation may lead to death as surely as a terminal disease that is diagnosed.

In Britain, too, work with dying people in the forerunners of the modern hospices was often charitable work with those who were destitute or social outcasts. Although welfare legislation has considerably altered the picture, recent years have seen the growth of an 'underclass'. 'Destitution' has been replaced by 'social exclusion' (Alcock 1998), and we have seen earlier that it is on this margin with those who are socially excluded that much social care exists (Parton 1996). In terms of Seale's definition of dying as 'falling from culture' (1998) which has individual and social as well as physical determinants, some of those living on the margins of society are living with social death, and there are clear links with the issue of social exclusion. Such exclusion may be seen as imposed or as 'chosen' by people who reject society. This includes those who are heavily involved in substance misuse and those who choose death through suicide, some of whom may live close to death (or to the idea of death) for a considerable time. For some, it is the 'project of the self', or aspects of social relations that begin the movement to death, rather than bodily deterioration.

Although these are theoretical issues that merit exploration, they will not be pursued further here. Bearing in mind its limitations, untimely adult deaths is used here to refer mainly to services for adults who have a medical diagnosis of a disease that is expected to result in death.

Social care workers who respond to their needs may be hospital, hospice or community based; if hospice based, they are likely to be specialists in palliative care; if community based, work with people who are dying may be only a part of their role. Examples are given from the work of each. In the light of points made above, the section on 'untimely adult deaths' ends with a look at social work with people who endanger their own lives through self-harm. Finally, I will look at work with those people described as 'elderly'.

To put these three sections into an overall perspective, it is worth remembering (see Table 3.1) that deaths over 28 days and under 19 years account for less than one per cent of annual deaths in England and Wales. Those between 20 and 64 years represent just under 16 per cent of all deaths, and deaths over 65 years, for just over 83 per cent (Office for National Statistics 2000).

5.1.1 Working with Children Facing Death

This century has witnessed a transformation in the patterns of death in childhood. Since my focus here is upon work with the child facing death, I shall exclude consideration of infant mortality, although this will be an important issue to consider when we look at bereavement. This leaves two main sets of circumstances in relation to those dying in childhood: those leading to death which is sudden or unexpected and those involving severe congenital disabilities, long-term degenerative conditions or malignancy. Such circumstances raise different issues in relation both to the time preceding death, and the child's experience, and for the survivors.

A high proportion (nearly 30 per cent: see Table 3.2) of deaths in those aged between 28 days old and 19 years are from external causes such as accidents of one kind or another. Such deaths are, by definition, unexpected. If death is not immediate, there may be a period of time when the child's condition is critical and death is a possibility. In such instances, the need for highly technical medical intervention is likely to be such that the child is in hospital throughout. Hospital social workers may be involved, together with other hospital workers, during the period of crisis for the child. The role of parents tends, of necessity, to be passive whilst medical staff try to save the child's life. It may be only in retrospect that the child is acknowledged to have been 'dying' rather than 'fighting for life'. In some instances, the child may survive but with long term consequences that transform their life experience to the extent that it resembles that of children with a life-threatening disease or long-term disability; a situation that is considered below.

Where an accident results in death that is instantaneous, there is an immediate transition from life to death, with no period of 'dying'. It is bereavement, rather than dying, that is the focus for care workers, although this grieving does start in the hospital environment, with the way in which the death is handled. Accounts by parents following the sudden or traumatic death of a child (e.g. Awoonor-Renner 1993; Jenkinson and Bodkin 1996) still indicate that staff may be more occupied with keeping things 'ordered' than with the needs of parents, although practices are changing. Examples are given in Chapter 8 of social workers – one hospital based, another community based – who took a lead in recognising the importance for survivors of what occurs at the time of death and immediately after it.

In a small (but highly publicised) number of instances, social workers are implicated in the death of a child. This may be from non-accidental injuries, which it is suggested that the worker might have prevented, or from accidents which are also seen to have been avoidable had the carer acted differently. The incidence of solvent abuse in young people in care gives considerable cause for concern. In 1990, an average of three people a week died as a result of sniffing solvents – the great majority of whom were young people between 13 and 18. One study in the 1970s and early 1980s found that death rates were ten times higher for young people in care than for others under 18 years old (Rickford 1992). Are such young people to be considered as 'dying'? Much attention has been paid to the abuse of children by others; less to issues of self-abuse.

The experience of children with a degenerative or life-threatening disease that will result in death before adulthood – estimated at 20,000 at any one time in the UK (Open University 1999) – is quite different. The report of a working party set up in 1987 (Thornes 1988) identified three groups of children as 'dying':

- Those with progressive degenerative conditions for which there is no current cure, such as muscular dystrophy, mucopolysaccharidosis, or cystic fibrosis.
- Those with a handicap which is so severe as to be a threat to life.
- Those with a life-threatening disease, such as leukaemia, liver disease or a profound heart malformation in which medical intervention may prove successful, but which still cause a sizeable number of deaths in childhood. (Thornes 1990: 162–3)

In some of these conditions, the child might lead a relatively normal life between periods of surgery or treatment; in others there will be ongoing treatment or deterioration. As for adults, the particular nature of the condition determines the dying trajectory (see above, section 3.7) and family expectations concerning the life expectancy of their child.

Mulkay and Ernst (1991) suggest that in the case of children who are dying, there is a reversal of the social death process (see above, section 3.2), with strenuous efforts to keep life as normal as possible for as long as possible. In the case of children who are dying, the family is very clearly the unit of care. Parents are the primary carers, and both specialist and mainstream services explicitly aim to support the family by providing respite and other care in the most flexible way possible.

Practical needs loom large in accounts of innovative services. For example, Cleary writes of the Rainbow Trust, that 'families where there is a terminally ill child need both holiday havens and extra pairs of hands in their home' (1990: 37). In the terms used in the last chapter, *managing the present* is, for these families, a full-time and exhausting business. Service initiatives have therefore sought to reduce this strain in ways that are acceptable and leave the parents in control. Siblings and the wider family are part of the picture in all services (Baum, Dominica and Woodward 1990).

Helen House, the first UK children's hospice, was opened in 1982. Since the 1980s, there has been considerable expansion of this work (compare, for example, Day 1990, with Notta in Oliviere *et al*. 1998: 148–54), and evaluation of it (Stein and Woolley 1990), of which social workers are part. Specialist social work posts have also been established. In 1999, there were 19 children's hospices open in Great Britain, with 145 beds (Hospice Information Service 1999). Many children who use these services have a severe disability.

Alongside specialist services for dying children are mainstream services for children with a disability. As one worker said, 'death is always on the agenda for parents with a severely disabled child'. Social services teams for children with a disability and educational services for severely disabled children have therefore worked for many years with a proportion of children and carers who are facing the death of a child. The head of care in one residential school spoke of the deaths of nearly a dozen children with whom she had been involved. In some instances, the death had actually occurred at school, either unexpectedly, or, in one case, in a planned way, the child having been cared for on a 24-hour basis in familiar school surroundings during his final decline, at the parents' request.

In one local authority, a specialist community team was set up in the early 1990s to respond to the needs of all children where there is profound lifelong disability. This is now a joint health and social services team, having undergone all the usual difficulties in establishing genuinely interdisciplinary ways of working (see also account of the early months of Acorns, in Birmingham: Day 1990). All cases handled by this team are long-term, and the social worker very often has the role of co-ordinator. Death is always an issue, and the family is likely to find it impossible to plan their lives. Various forms of respite care are available, accessed through the team, and this is a crucial area of care for this group of service users. Stein and Woolley (1990) report the preliminary findings of a study that investigated families' perceptions both of respite care and of community services. Extreme variation was found, both in the availability and quality of services. Moreover, as a child's condition deteriorated, a form of respite care that had been helpful (such as a link scheme) might no longer be usable.

5.1.2   Untimely Adult Deaths

Writing in 1982, Smith could, in her text on social work with the dying and bereaved (Smith 1982: 60), concentrate almost exclusively upon work by hospital-based social workers with patients dying in hospital. Hospice care is not discussed, yet this hospital-based social work role was the crucible from which specialist psychosocial palliative care (Sheldon 1997; Oliviere *et al.* 1998; Monroe 1998) was to grow. Social workers whose careers span these 20 years describe the development from a generic hospital-based role which included work with some patients who were dying, to the establishment of specialist community or hospital-based teams for those who were terminally ill and the growth of hospice care. Later, there was the establishment of further specialist teams for those with AIDS.

Specialist Services

In 1999, in the UK and the Republic of Northern Ireland, there were the following specialist services:

- 3,342 specialist beds for dying people in voluntary and NHS settings;
- 347 hospitals with support teams or a support nurse;

- about 370 specialist home care teams (the approximation is because of difficulties in defining a 'team');
- 250 day hospices. (Hospice Information Service 1999)

These figures include in-patient units for children (19 with 145 beds), and 3 dedicated units for people with HIV/AIDS with 74 beds. In 1995, Sheldon reported that there were over 200 specialist social workers (Sheldon 1995). According to Brodribb and Smith (1995), about one in four specialist social workers were employed by social services departments, and three-quarters in the voluntary sector. The number of hospice beds is increasing (by over 200 in the past 4 years, with day hospices up by an extra 25 per cent over figures in 1995). Half the admissions result in discharge and although the average length of stay remains fairly constant, services are being provided for a greater range and greater numbers of dying patients.

Hospice care is tremendously varied, depending upon whether the unit is independently or NHS funded and whether it has a particular religious affiliation, as well as upon the personalities and circumstances that have shaped its individual development. Listening to social workers from such settings, there is often a strong sense that the social work role is being developed and created by the workers themselves in negotiation with other staff. The credibility both of the individuals and of the social work contribution in the particular institution may well depend on their ability to work with other professionals and establish a distinctive but complementary role. Thus, for example, not all specialist social workers undertake statutory community care assessments; although those employed by the local authority are likely to do so. It is often the case that the non-specialist community-based worker will take the role of care manager since care plans need to span more than one short-term period of admission.

Given such variation, examples of specialist work with dying people cannot be taken as representative. More detail of the enormous range of work that is undertaken under the umbrella of specialist psychosocial palliative care can be found in recent dedicated texts such as Sheldon (1997) and Oliviere, Hargreaves and Monroe (1998). Brodribb and Smith (1995), Harrison (1996) and Brewer (1996) all give short accounts of their role as specialist social workers in hospice settings. The examples in this present book are taken from interviews with workers from a large, religiously based in-patient unit with community outreach programme, a smaller rural independently funded hospice and a voluntarily funded day centre in the grounds of an NHS hospital, employing a seconded local authority social worker. Social workers in these settings offer a secondary level of service. Much of the routine psychosocial care is done by the nursing team in the course of caring for patients. Social work tends to focus upon the interface between the unit and the community, either helping to draw up care plans or liasing with those outside the unit who do so. With in-patients, social workers may be called in where psychosocial care needs more time than that available from those who are concerned with physical care, or where nurses feel out of their depth or the patient feels a need to speak with someone outside the routines of ongoing physical care.

■ Alice Brown is an in-patient in the hospice. As her physical health deteriorates, she is becoming increasingly withdrawn. Nurses' attempts to discuss her situation with her meet with no success. Her teenaged son is finding visits difficult, as he does not know what to say. His mother speaks as though she will be there in the future, but he knows that she is aware that she will not be. A member of the social work team becomes involved.

Admission to an in-patient unit can involve considerable loss of privacy and a lack of boundaries, especially where the emphasis is upon holistic care. The social worker has a somewhat separate identity and can also cross the boundary between the institution and life at home. He or she may be able to help a person to deal with issues that are broader than those involved in physical care, such as those concerning the future of dependants, or putting the person's affairs in order through healing past breaches in family relations.

■ Joshua is from Sierra Leone. He is a quiet man who was in Britain for a year with a return air ticket, when the war prevented his return. He has no benefits, and his family of a wife, children and mother are all in Sierra Leone. Now that he has a terminal illness, his one wish is to return home to die. In the hospice, he has an air of bewilderment. A social worker is asked to see him on the ward.

Particular provision has been made for social work with people who are diagnosed as HIV positive or who have AIDS. Such posts have been funded largely by special grants from the Department of Health.

The need for such specialist services is justified by the continued discrimination and stigmatisation associated with AIDS, which means that those affected still do not have real access to mainstream services. In practical terms, this means that all work with these particular service users must be much more detailed; home carers need to be selected and properly trained if confidentiality and an adequate standard of care are to be offered. At present, specialist posts mean that work can be more holistic, and a very broad range of services can be provided. This range is illustrated in the examples below.

- Simon is HIV-positive. He is white, and well educated with a responsible job, a reasonable income and good accommodation. No one knows about his diagnosis, and he wishes to keep it this way. He has access to the services of the social worker, who is part of the local specialist team based at the hospital.

- Jane is a white woman who is a single parent; she has been jailed for a drugs offence. She is HIV positive and in touch with the local clinic team.

- Robert's infidelity became known when his diagnosis was revealed when he became seriously ill. He and his wife gave the appearance of being a conventional middle-class white couple. His wife responded to his condition and what it revealed by refusing access to their home.

- Grace, a 52-year-old black Ugandan refugee who left four children, her husband and her extended family when she fled political violence, became ill; she was diagnosed as having pneumonia and discovered to be HIV positive. The social worker from the specialist team was involved.

The social work response to these situations is outlined in the next section. Thanks to dramatic changes in medical treatment, numbers on the caseload of such specialist workers are rising, as survival rates improve dramatically. This has led in some instances to a different range of problems when some people are living much longer than they expected. The role of such a specialist worker is much more like that of hospital social workers in the 1980s or the hospice social worker of today, with full integration into a multi-disciplinary team, and scope to offer a broad range of services in response to whatever needs are jointly identified.

Mainstream Services

Looking now from the perspective of mainstream community social care services, social care workers from adult teams – often those whose remit covers people with a disability – receive referrals from hospitals and hospices and seek to respond to some of the needs of those who are 'sent home to die'. In some instances, a specialist social worker will continue to be involved; more often, the community worker takes on the case – either from the point of discharge planning or after initial arrangements have been established by the specialist in-patient team. The following examples give an idea of the work of social workers in adult fieldwork teams.

■ A referral has been received relating to Mr Wilson, a man in his 50s currently in hospital, but due for discharge home as soon as possible. He has terminal cancer and is not expected to live more than a few months. His wife Olive is herself in poor health, their children do not live nearby and she is very worried about caring for him at home. As a result of his illness, their income is now much reduced.

■ Mumtaz Bibi is 27-years-old, originally from Pakistan, and has four young children. She is expected to live about a year. She is cared for at home by her sister-in-law Saira, who shares a house with her and with their two husbands, who are brothers. The school has expressed concern about the very withdrawn behaviour and frequent absences from school of the youngest child. A request has been made for a community care assessment.

■ John's partner Karen wanted to care for him at home in his final months, but also wanted to keep her part-time job as she knew that this would be really important to her after his death. The care plan needed to work around her working hours.

As well as some who are terminally ill, a large proportion of the service users with whom social workers from such teams work have a steadily deteriorating condition such as multiple sclerosis. This disease has been suggested as an example of Glaser and Strauss's second dying trajectory – 'certain death at an unknown time' (see above, section 3.7). For most, gradual decline leads to a focus upon coping with the disability rather than to seeing themselves as 'dying', but for some there can be a very strong sense of increasing social exclusion.

■ Matthew is a white man who has multiple sclerosis. Increasing disability has led to the loss of his job, and with it his status as breadwinner as well as loss of mobility. Members of his family have moved away and now see him only at weekends. Initially he went from one consultant to another looking for a more favourable diagnosis. He is experiencing a gradual marginalisation from society, and says that life is a 'senseless routine based around the time schedule of my carers'.

Home carers, where needed, may be employed by local authorities or by private agencies under contract to the Local Authority. Together with District Nurses, they may help with practical aspects of the care of people who are terminally ill at home.

■ Margaret is a home carer who works on a part-time basis. Her caseload includes a number of younger clients with a severe disability or terminal illness. She identifies easily with Susan, a woman of about her own age who has cancer, and finds it easy to be tempted to go beyond her designated hours in trying to help. Susan seems to find it easier to talk to Margaret about her illness than to her husband, who thinks that they should both try to keep cheerful for the sake of the children. Everyone says that Susan is very brave.

The work of home carers and of the care managers or care co-ordinators, who put together packages of care for people who are dying at home, is often unrecognised in a public sense. For example, newspaper tributes after a death often thank doctors and nurses, but rarely home carers or social workers. Research studies too may give the impression of little, or even negatively perceived, involvement (see, for example, comments made by GPs, in Field 1998). Yet social care workers themselves speak of the 'privilege' of working with people who have been 'sent home to die', and private letters of thanks from relatives received by such carers belie their omission from public testimonials. There seems to be something of a disjuncture between public evaluations of service and private ones. Sometimes this is because the service user – or another interested party – is disappointed in either the range or the nature of services offered. In cases where this is not so, and where services are welcomed, their very acceptability can mean that workers are told 'you're not really like a social worker'. This is meant as a compliment, and reflects the negative public image of much of social care, and people's wish to distance themselves from it. In the case of home care, if the carer is liked she becomes known by name, not role.

Mental Health Services and the Issue of Self-Harm

Community mental health services, and the social care workers who are members of them, work with people for whom their own identity and continued existence may seem to be undesirable or problematic. There are various ways in which this may manifest itself; through eating disorders, substance misuse or deliberate self-harm. The most extreme example is attempted or successful suicide, but all these activities do bring risk of biological death.

In large general hospitals, there is likely to be a social worker employed by social services as part of a specialist psychiatric team responding to incidents of self-harm. The social work role is to assess those patients who have been admitted following self-harm, and to do initial follow-up where necessary. Some will be already under a psychiatrist, and therefore perhaps clients of other colleagues in the community mental health team; others are not known to the psychiatric services prior to the attempt. The first task is to differentiate suicidal attempt (where there is a serious wish to die) from self-harm (where there may not be). One such worker says that her work differs from most of social care in that this kind of despair affects people from all walks of life. There are, however, gender differences in the seriousness of attempts (men's attempts are more serious) and wish for help (women are more likely to want and use help). For some, the crisis itself brings about a measure of resolution. This worker, a trained psychotherapist, offers counselling to those who want it and will, in her view, benefit from it. For the overwhelming majority of those people she sees, there is a link with the experience of significant early loss. Other studies of depression (e.g. Brown and Harris 1978) have also made this link, which is often with bereavement in childhood.

5.1.3   Services for Older People: Facing Deterioration and Death

In the UK, roughly half of those people aged over 85 years receive some form of care from social services departments, and the greatest need for services for older people comes in the year before death, whatever their age (Douglas and Philpot 1998: 96). Even when they are not seen to be 'dying' therefore, a large proportion of the elderly people who are in touch with social care workers will in fact be close to death.

In the case of older people, awareness of dying is often not a matter of specific disclosure or of deception; it is a much more general issue. Some older people may seem preoccupied with thoughts of death – turning first to the obituaries in the paper or talking about contemporaries who have died or wishing for their own demise. Others do not refer to it, and seem almost to ignore the deaths of fellow residents in care homes, for example. As we have already seen, much of the literature about dying concerns issues of disclosure, and concentrates on the hospital context. How, if at all, does this apply to the social care of older people, often in community rather than hospital settings?

Assessment

Age-related disability and social isolation are the factors that have been identified as associated with a need for social care services (Douglas and Philpot 1998). These factors are interrelated – change in a person's level of dependency may mean that living alone is no longer possible, or may result in informal carers being unable to continue to manage. Either way, a referral is likely to be made for an assessment under the NHS and Community Care Act 1990. Social workers and others undertaking such assessments are centrally involved therefore in decisions about where individuals will live, and where they will die. This is not to deny that overall patterns and possibilities are determined by policies way out of the control of individual workers or their clients. These include factors such as the growing numbers of people in older age groups and shifts in responsibilities between health and social services departments. At the local level such matters result in strict eligibility criteria for services, and in negotiations between home carers and district nurses about the boundaries of care.

Social workers or care managers (not all of whom are social workers) are the people who interpret such policies in individual cases. Their role is therefore pivotal, yet often seems to be reduced to an almost mechanical measuring of extensive needs against dwindling services. Asking such workers about their ability to respond to grief in a service user, aware that this decision which is ostensibly about where they will live is actually about where they will die, is likely to meet with some resistance. Nevertheless, the assessment task is critical and can incorporate much sensitivity to these issues if the worker allows this to happen. We will look at this when we consider the worker's response, below.

The following scenarios hint at the complexities that are likely to be part of the assessment role.

■ Mrs Porter, a white woman of 80 in hospital is referred to the social worker for arrangements to be made for discharge following admission after a fall at home. She is frail and has poor eyesight. She was admitted from her own home where her daughter visited daily. She wants to return home and considers herself able to manage with help from her daughter as before. Since the death of her husband, she has tended not to go out and now has few friends or visitors. The daughter tells the social worker (but not in the first instance her mother) that she is no longer prepared to offer this level of support, and that her mother requires more help than she can provide. Her own partner has a drink problem and her son has recently been convicted of a minor offence. The hospital is pressing for immediate discharge.

■ Mr Jones is 75-years-old and has lived alone ever since the death of his wife ten years before. They had no children. He has always been an active member of the British Legion club, where he is well known. Over a period of months, he begins to attend less regularly and there is an observable deterioration in his physical appearance, which has always been meticulous in the past. One day he is abusive towards another member. A concerned neighbour rings the social services department after having failed to see Mr Jones out and about for several days. Mr Jones refuses to admit the worker when she calls to conduct an assessment, and there is concern that he may be at risk. When she does gain admittance, with the help of the police, they find open, festering cans of half-eaten food littering the living room and other signs of a lack of physical self care. After a physical check by his GP, which reveals only minor physical weaknesses, Mr Jones agrees to admit the care manager to conduct an assessment of his needs on the following day.

Seale (1996) describes the way in which older people attempt to maintain a reputation for independence. Regimes of self-care and personal hygiene, of cleanliness and order in the house and of reciprocity in relationships are the markers of such independence recognised by lay people as well as professionals. Failure to maintain these projects is indeed realised to be the onset of social death. As such, many, like Mr Jones, 'prefer to mark the beginning of their social deaths by resisting help' (Seale 1998: 156).

As described in Chapter 3, dying is, in Seale's analysis, a falling from culture that has bodily, emotional and social aspects. In the case of untimely adult deaths, the dominant revivalist script (see above, section 3.4) emphasises awareness and the psychological processes involved in realising that death is imminent. In the case of older people, awareness is a more rounded process in which psychological reactions may be less prominent than the painstaking endeavour to resist and delay providing others with evidence of what is known to be inevitable. It is often a social worker or care manager who is associated with the acknowledgement that this attempt is no longer sustainable. At the point of discharge from hospital, many aged persons have to accept that they are no longer able to live independently. This is, in a very real sense, a critical juncture in the process towards 'social death' (see above, section 3.2, for a discussion of this concept). Yet the community care assessment is not described in terms of the disclosure of a diagnosis of social death. Perhaps is should be seen in this way. It is ironic that at a time when there is a demand for better communication on the part of doctors who inform patients that they are dying (Buckman 1984, 1998; Maguire and Faulkner 1988), there is pressure for the process of making arrangements for this kind of social change (which is usually negatively perceived, however good the institutional care) quickly and as part of a routinised practical process. Social workers are likely to find it hard to resist such pressures especially if they experience a lack of understanding and support from their managers in doing so.

Care at Home

A package or plan of care that enables a person to stay at home is one of the outcomes that may follow assessment by a social worker or care manager. It is important to remember, however, that family members in fact provide the majority of home care. Home carers may supplement their work or, in the case of those who live alone, may be members of a multi-disciplinary home care team who offer continuing care.

In 1996, nearly 500,000 households in England and Wales received home care services (DoH 1996). In a very real sense, such workers are working with dying people on a daily basis, helping them to get up, to dress and go to the toilet, to heat meals perhaps provided by a meals service and to feed themselves.

■ Doreen was 93-years-old. Her husband died many years ago; they had no children. She lived alone. Her nephew came when he could. She could do very little for herself. A carer came in two or three times a day, seven days a week, for two and a half hours at a time. The home carers gave her a bath, made the bed, got her meals and washed up. Then Doreen would sit in her chair and sleep until the next carer came to put her to bed. She was more or less totally deaf, with poor eyesight and very frail. She communicated by writing notes, which often said 'Why am I still here? Why can't I die?' She died three days after entering a nursing home.

Deterioration and approaching death may be very apparent to the carer, if not to the service user, and it is not unusual for it to be the home carer who discovers that a client has died.

A home carer telephones the care manager to say that she cannot raise a reply from a client. She is an elderly, frail lady whom the carer has visited for many years. The manager calls the police, and the carer calls back later to say that the service user was found to be dead when they broke into the house. (Currer 1992: 158)

Most people express a preference for remaining in their own homes until they die (Townsend *et al.* 1990). Current policies state that their aim is to enable people to live (and presumably die) in their own homes where possible (Department of Health 1989). Where it is possible for this to occur, those caring for the dying are, in the case of elderly people, either informal family carers or health and social care workers such as district nurses and home carers, as well as staff working in day centres. Whilst community nurses are professionally trained, home carers have little training. Increasingly the agencies providing such services are private agencies. The responsibility for specifying and maintaining standards of service is, however, with those who purchase such services from these agencies – usually the local authority social services department. The same is true of the other group of carers who provide hands-on daily care for older people who are dying – care assistants in residential homes.

Residential Care of Older People

In 1993, 12–15 per cent of all deaths occurred in residential and nursing homes (Field and James 1993: 17). Over the twenty years up to 1994, admission figures more than doubled (Laing and Buisson 1995). This rise was considerably accelerated by a planned decline in hospital long-stay provision and the changes brought about by the NHS and Community Care Act 1990. Private sector provision now far outstrips public provision, although responsibility for inspection and registration of homes remains a matter for statutory authorities. It has been estimated that a quarter of all people over 85 years live in a residential home setting of some kind (Sidell, Katz and Komaromy 1998).

There have been two recent studies of death and dying in this setting. A small-scale study by Shemmings (1996) reports interviews with 20 carers in 5 homes. Sidell, Katz and Komaromy (1998) conducted a much more comprehensive national study, which included a survey of 1,000 residential and nursing homes in England and interviews with 100 heads of residential and nursing homes. This study has yielded a valuable profile of the residents in the homes that responded to the survey. Residents were mainly female (three times as many women as men), predominantly widowed, and many had lived in the home for a considerable time. Just under a quarter (21 per cent) had lived in the home over five years, with a further third (35 per cent) having lived there between 2 and 5 years. Very few residents (1 per cent) from the surveyed homes were from a minority ethnic group.

The study's authors note two implications of this profile. Firstly, as widows, death has already touched many residents' lives closely, possibly involving them in having cared for a terminally ill partner. Secondly, as long-stay residents, relationships will have been formed with staff and fellow residents. These factors have implications for their awareness of death, and for the impact of deaths upon others in the homes. The authors suggest that 'about 32,000 old people die in residential care in England and Wales annually' (Sidell, Katz and Komaromy 1998: 3). In residential homes, the study found a death rate of 16 per cent; this figure was higher in nursing homes, which admit people who are more physically frail or ill. Over half of those who died were over 85 years. 'General deterioration' was the most frequently cited cause of death. Despite a wish to enable all residents to remain in the home until death, just under a third of those in residential homes did in fact die in hospital, following transfer from the home.

Drawing both on my own interviews and on those reported by Sidell *et al.* (1998), we can see that good deaths are those that are predictable and planned, and where staff members know the resident and their family's wishes and can follow these, as in the following example.

■ There is a change in the behaviour and demeanour of a long-stay resident; an almost catatonic state, with altered breathing. Care staff tell the manager on duty that they do not think it will be long before she dies. The relatives have already discussed with the manager where they can be reached and at what times of day. They are alerted, and visit the following day. As expected, she does die three days later.

By contrast, difficult deaths are unpredictable. Often, this means they are sudden, as in the following example.

■ A short-stay resident is found on the floor of the sitting-room. Care staff fear that the person may be dead, and call the duty manager. Other residents are apparently unconcerned.

It is unpredictability, rather than just the suddenness of a death, that is the main problem for staff. The following unusual example illustrates what may happen when an anticipated death does not occur.

■ One lady has been resident for six years. On admission, the doctor did not expect her to live two weeks. She has terrible attacks when she seems to die and then comes back spontaneously. She wants to die, has been ready for many years, and is very angry when she comes round from her attacks. At first, there was satisfaction for staff in keeping her alive; then satisfaction that she had come to terms with death and was no longer afraid; now they are sad for her. Her family are supportive but withdrawing. Although still visiting, they are less anxious as the years go on.

Other deaths defined by staff as unsatisfactory are those that follow a transfer out of the home into hospital or nursing care. This leads to a sense of having failed in the aim of enabling the resident to die in the home where they were known – a regret perhaps very similar to that of some family members at the earlier point of admission to residential care. Deaths shortly after admission are also difficult, because relationships have yet to be established with the resident and any family (Siddell, Katz and Komaromy 1998: 115). A more extreme example of this, not mentioned in Siddell *et al.*'s research, occurs where a unit offers respite care and a short-stay resident dies unexpectedly, as in the example given above. That example also illustrates another category of deaths that trouble staff – those that occur in a communal area or require investigation because they are very sudden.

All the homes, in both studies, sought to ensure that a dying person was not left alone (Shemmings 1996; Siddell, Katz and Komaromy 1998). This accords with views of neighbours reported in community studies (Seale 1995). In practice, Sidell and colleagues report that this aim is not always achieved. Finally, they found that staff members were disturbed by those deaths where the resident was seen to be suffering or in pain. The GPs who served the residential homes in their study varied greatly in their knowledge of issues of effective pain control in terminal illness, and it is one of the report's recommendations that this situation be improved.

It is clear that the ability to define and to predict death is significant and has implications for care. In the case of older people, this can be problematic (Blackburn 1989; Seale 1991; George and Sykes 1997). In residential homes, regimes of care, amounts of staff attention and decisions about transfer (if death is thought close, this will be avoided, even for a resident needing a lot of care) are all affected by the ability to predict imminent death.

In residential care of older people, then, death and dying are part of the job. In Sidell, Katz and Komaromy's study, 50 per cent of Local Authority Homes had staff with a social work qualification (1998: 130) – this would usually be the Head of Home. Some report important differences between their approach and a nursing or medical approach, also between a social work qualification and training in management, which is becoming a preferred option in some places. We look next at what does distinguish social care.

5.2   The Social Care Response

Given the diversity of situations in which social care workers are involved with people who are close to death, are there themes or commonalties that can be identified across this wide range of roles? Here I identify and illustrate five strands that were seen, by the practitioners whom I interviewed, to be important elements in their work. They were not all necessarily the attributes exclusively of social care; indeed, some others who were working in this area (such as a hospital chaplain, a trainer, a nurse) mentioned one or other aspect as important for anyone working with dying people. Together, however, they represent a range of characteristics that can be seen as necessary for 'good practice' and they offer a useful way of thinking about the service that social care workers are seeking to offer. Each is illustrated with reference to the responses of the workers involved in one or more of the examples given in the previous section, in order to show clearly how these aspects of care are manifest in practice.

5.2.1   A Response that is Both Emotional and Practical

As we saw in Chapter 2, the duality of practical assistance and emotional support is widely seen to be characteristic of social care generally, and most workers claimed that in this respect, work with dying people was no different from other areas of social care. Working together on some of the practical aspects of a service user's situation can give the client time to assess whether they are prepared to broach more difficult emotional issues with the worker. This was evident in work with Joshua in the hospice setting, with Jane in prison and with Robert following the loss of his home when he was diagnosed as having AIDS.

- Joshua was at first unwilling to discuss emotional issues with anyone, maintaining a blandly polite response to all enquiries. As time went on, however, he worked with the social worker on plans for his return to Sierra Leone, starting to speak of his distress at having left his family there, and his fears that he might not be well enough to go back and see them before he died.

- In relation to Jane, the specialist social worker was faced with making practical arrangements for the care of her children, seeking to prevent loss of her accommodation through loss of housing benefits whilst she was in prison, and also questions about the availability of appropriate medical care in jail. Jane communicated her anger and emotional turmoil in letters from prison to the social worker, whom she seemed to trust. The worker visited her on a regular basis until her release.

- In Robert's case accommodation suitable for a seriously ill man had to be found very quickly, and equipped from scratch. This was not just a practical matter, but had to be done whilst he was still coming to terms with the fact of all that he had lost.

Many workers stressed the interrelatedness of practical arrangements and emotional reactions: 'You can't think about death if you are worried about debt' was the way one person put it. Putting the same argument another way round, another experienced practitioner pointed to the emotional aspects of apparently practical tasks. Claiming attendance allowance or other benefits is not just about filling in the forms, she said. Often you have first to help people to get over the emotional hurdle of accepting that their situation is such that they are eligible. You must work through and acknowledge the emotional issues before you can work on practical tasks. Many workers spoke of a danger that it is becoming increasingly hard for workers in mainstream social care to hold these two aspects together; current policy seems to be to reduce the assessment of care needs to a practical matter that can be completed quickly and by minimally qualified workers.

We have seen that in services for children with a life-threatening disability, practical matters are immensely important and often the basis of service responses. 'Managing the present' in practical terms is the first priority. Once this becomes tolerable, parents and dying people themselves may be able to deal with emotional matters. In relation to services for those who harm themselves, this balance is the other way round. Emotional matters are a priority as it is these that threaten the desire to survive. Until the person can relinquish their abandonment of their own future, the present holds little meaning.

5.2.2 Being There: The 'Gift of Presence' and Dependability

A number of workers emphasised that it was important that service users found them reliable. Others spoke of being alongside the service user. This seemed to be an emotional, practical and structural issue. At its simplest, it was a matter of just being there, of offering company and companionship. There were many examples, but all seemed to be in 'out of duty time'. Thus a teacher spoke of her vigil with parents sitting by a dying teenager. Care assistants came into the residential home where they worked to sit with a dying resident when they were off duty. Clearly, this was seen as important, but equally clearly most working hours did not allow for it. At another level, however, this also included the importance of conveying a sense of reliability. Thus one social worker spoke of the anxieties that many people feel when faced with the prospect of caring for a terminally ill partner or relative at home. Hospital has felt safe, because there is always someone on hand, but there are many unknowns to be faced at home, from the carer's perspective. An experienced worker who has a fairly clear idea of the services that they are likely to be able to offer can discuss these anxieties before the patient is discharged, and address some of the 'what if . . . ' questions of their carer.

■ When the community social worker saw Mr Wilson and his wife in hospital before his discharge, she was able to ascertain that his wife Olive was most worried about how she would cope if he were unwell during the night. She was able to let her know that although they could not cover every night, it was likely that a sitting service could be arranged on a regular basis, and that together with input from the district nurses, a way could be worked out of spreading the load. She was also able to identify some benefits to which the couple would be entitled, which would ease her financial worries.

The role of the care manager is, in this worker's view, to be dependable and to enable someone to have a reasonable death at home without too many anxieties. Anxieties on the part of the carer are easily transmitted to the dying person, impeding the coping of both. The experience and confidence of the worker is an important element in this. In the same way, the manager of a residential home saw her role as being the one that staff and relatives could rely on. It was important to have clear policies and procedures to follow in case of a death. This contributed to a sense of security for staff, residents and relatives. In relation to work with parents of children with a life-threatening illness, dependability and reliability are critical. Without these qualities, even the best service is no use. For a different reason, service users who are HIV+ or have AIDS need to be able to rely on the confidentiality and consistency of service responses. 'Trust, confidentiality and reliability are of critical importance in the practice of any individual or agency providing support' (Davies 1995: 41).

5.2.3   Offering Time and Attention; Listening

This was evident in almost all the accounts, and was the single factor most emphasised by specialist and mainstream workers alike. In the in-patient hospice situation, Alice Brown found that she could begin to move on when she had had a chance to express her own fears. In this case, it was important to offer her the opportunity to meet the social worker away from the ward situation.

■   The ward staff and social worker agree that it might be helpful for her to see Alice away from the ward situation, where she has become increasingly withdrawn. A wheelchair is arranged and they walk in the garden. As she introduces herself, Alice gradually begins to speak of the death of her own mother, which occurred when she was in her teens. Her main memory is of her embarrassment when her mother broke down in a public place. Alice feels very exposed on the open ward. She is determined to keep face in front of the nurses and other patients, and not to lose control. She wants her son's memories of her to be good ones. She is afraid that she will not be able to be as brave for his sake as she wants to be. She is surprised to learn that he has similar fears. Reflecting on her own experience, she wishes that she had been able to speak to her mother before she died. The practitioner suggests a number of ways to break the silence that has developed between Alice and her son. Alice decides to write him a letter that he can read at home in private, and then to meet him in the garden on his next visit. Unfortunately, she dies unexpectedly before this meeting takes place, but not before she has managed to write to him. The staff on the ward report that, although still very reticent, Alice seemed much more peaceful once she had done this.

In some cases, as with Simon, a listening ear is all that is needed. He makes an appointment with the social worker to 'offload' some of his stress from time to time. It is a relief to be able to talk to someone who is fully aware of his diagnosis.

For Mumtaz, the situation is more complicated but still involves seeking to understand not only her feelings, but also those of her husband and sister-in-law. The worker's first task is to arrange for an interpreter who can speak to both women in their own language. Once this has been arranged, the situation becomes clearer, and some aspects of it can be resolved.

■ Saira, Mumtaz's sister-in-law, resents the extra work involved in caring for Mumtaz's children as well as her own and in doing her share of the housework. There are nine children under 10 years at home altogether, some of whom are not yet of school age. Mumtaz, meanwhile, feels completely useless and excluded, and that her children are increasingly turning to Saira, who treats them less well than her own children. She says that she might as well already be dead. She has responded by spending increasing amounts of time in prayer, and by keeping her youngest child with her whenever possible. The social worker is able to offer some help in the house to ease the burden on Saira and assisted nursery places for two of the younger children. Saira is encouraged to give Mumtaz simple jobs to do, rather than leaving her alone. The benefits of this for Mumtaz are explained to Mumtaz's husband, who has had a tendency to expect Saira, as his younger brother's wife, to do more for Mumtaz than is strictly necessary. Mumtaz accepts that it is better for her youngest child to continue to attend school, rather than staying home with her.

As a home carer, Margaret's role with Susan is ostensibly a practical one, but her ability to listen to Susan is just as important as the housework she does, enabling her to become an important source of emotional support. This is partly because Susan does not see her as a 'professional', and because she comes to the house regularly when both her husband and children are out at work or school. Susan does not feel that she has to 'keep up appearances' with Margaret. It would have been quite possible for Margaret to have done the housework in a way that did not facilitate the establishment of such a supportive relationship. She might, for example, have taken the approach of trying to divert Susan or to 'cheer her up' or 'jolly her along' rather than listening to her. Recognising the importance of simply listening is essential but often not as easy as it looks.

In the cases of Mr Jones and of Mrs Porter and her daughter, the opportunity to express fears led to an acknowledgement of what might actually be possible, as follows:

- The immediate need in Mrs Porter's situation was to establish whether she would be able to manage at home, what level of support would be necessary, and where this might come from. Talking about her own difficulties seemed to free her daughter up to consider whether she might be able to visit twice a week if a home carer did the housework and shopping on the other days. The social worker looked into the benefits that could be payable and suggested that it might be good to offer some periods of respite care in a local residential home with a view to later admission if Mrs Porter was unable to manage at home. The daughter's main fear was of being trapped, but as they looked at the various options, she started to cry. She told the worker how much she wanted to continue to be involved in caring for her mother, as she felt she had 'made a mess of everything else in my life'.

- Mr Jones starts the assessment by asserting that he would rather die than leave the house he shared with his wife. Whilst he is there, he can still talk to her as he used to. The care assessor agrees that leaving his home is not desirable, and asks what he finds most difficult at present. He admits that he is not eating well, and agrees to accept a cooked meal on weekdays. He is at first resistant to have 'some slip of a girl tidying my things' but eventually agrees to a weekly clean if this will mean that he can stay at home for the time being. He admits that he feels a bit ashamed of the state the house is in. He finds walking to the meetings of the British Legion difficult, but has not liked to be a 'bother' by asking for a lift. He agrees to the social worker contacting the local secretary, who is glad to make arrangements for Mr Jones to be picked up once a month.

For Mr Jones, social death has been temporarily postponed, although the social worker is aware that this may be only a short-term respite, as Mr Jones is showing some signs of dementia which will eventually make it impossible for him to live at home alone. For the time being, however, improved diet and some restored social activity improve his situation and the home carer is able to reduce the risk of accidental self-harm and monitor the situation.

Although in these two instances the outcome was that the service users were, for the time being, enabled to stay at home, this is not always the case. Nonetheless, when people are offered the opportunity to express their fears and are properly listened to as part of such an assessment, they will themselves often accept the necessity for changes that they have been dreading. Indeed, one worker argues that one of the most important aspects of working with people who have a terminal condition is in helping them to give up long-held assumptions about being able to live independently. Dying involves letting go of roles and relationships as well as slowing down physically. Sometimes this can be an opportunity to focus upon oneself for the first time. There is a need to accept limitations that are imposed by the illness.

More than anything else, say most of the workers I have spoken to, people need an ear, they need your time and attention. Even amidst the radically changed working situation of those social workers doing community care assessments, the ability to listen and to draw out people's fears and concerns is an essential aspect of the assessment task. Without this, it is not possible to sort out an appropriate package of care. For the social care worker who is providing services (such as home care) rather than having a purchasing role, listening is just as important.

5.2.4   Encouraging and Helping Communication with Others

Often it is important not only to listen to the service user but to help them to communicate more effectively with those close to them. This is an aspect of the social work role in specialist settings that is identified by Monroe (1998). We have already seen an example of this in the case of Alice Brown and her son. One worker told the story of an elderly man in a day centre who was dying but unable to communicate with his wife. He had been a keen gardener, and was helped by staff in the centre to make a miniature garden, which he gave to her. On another occasion, the same worker sat with the family of a dying teenager for two days. The father felt almost incapable of speaking to the silent body in the bed that was still his daughter. When eventually he did so, she responded 'almost as if she had been waiting'. The practitioner is convinced that his speaking to her had 'given her permission to die'. In the case of Grace, the social worker was able to explore with her questions of who she might tell of her HIV diagnosis. She decided eventually to confide in her vicar and members of the church, who responded in a very supportive way. In a situation where members of her own family were many miles away in Africa, this link became extremely important to her.

In services for children who are dying, one of the things that parents most value is the opportunity to talk to parents who have a child with a similar condition. An organisation called 'Contact a Family' exists to link parents, as well as to offer an information, advice and support service for professionals (a contact address is given at the end of this book).

5.2.5   Advocacy and a Challenge to Orthodoxy: Keeping the Focus on the Individual

The last of the themes to emerge from practitioner interviews concerns the role of the social care worker as advocate. This may well include challenging professional orthodoxies, including one's own, in order to keep the focus upon the individual service user and their particular needs. One worker spoke of accompanying the parents of a severely disabled child to hospital to collect supplies necessary for his care, and of challenging the bureaucracy that added to the parents' distress as each time a new doctor took the case history afresh. She also spoke with disgust of meetings at which workers sought to distinguish between what such parents wanted in terms of services, and what they 'really' needed. In face of enormous difficulties, she said, 'they ask for so little'. In her view, it is up to the professionals working alongside them to seek to remove obstacles to the care of their child.

Another worker saw her role as care manager as one that involved continually pushing out the boundaries of what could be offered in any instance. In the 1980s, a successful campaign was launched by a social worker to alter the restrictive rules concerning attendance allowance. This is an example of the way in which social care workers can seek to influence the development of services. A wider awareness of issues of social policy is part of the context that social carers offer and there are often opportunities to be involved with policy-making groups at the local level. Other professionals such as nurses have a perspective that is more closely focussed upon the individual; social workers bring an awareness of the extent to which the social context impacts on this experience. They should continually challenge restrictions, on the basis of their knowledge of the needs of service users (Monroe 1998). In this way, they can act as advocates at both an individual and a general level.

Some emphasised that the social care model is different from the medical model, and sometimes conflicts with it. It is not about treatment or 'making things better'. Often it is about accepting ambiguity, and helping people to accept limitation. The social work role is about being with people through troubled times, not necessarily comforting or pacifying them, but helping them to struggle to their own solutions. To do this, it is necessary to stay with people where they are, in both an emotional and practical sense (Monroe 1998). Most workers were very wary of theoretical models that proposed a way in which people 'ought' to respond to their situation. Their emphasis upon individuality was almost a creed. Care and care plans had to be driven by the service user. This did not mean that services were unlimited. One difficult but important skill was to tell people that resources were limited and that certain facilities could not be offered. It is possible to refuse a service without making the person feel rejected, should this be necessary, insisted one specialist worker. Most stressed that service users were entitled to honesty, both as individuals and as a group, about reductions in services where these existed. This should not be distorted by pretending that their need did not exist, just because no services were available to meet it. Practitioners need to support claims for adequate services, even where these cannot be provided.

5.2.6   Discussion

The three factors identified in Chapter 2 as characterising social care are all apparent in these accounts of work with service users who are close to death. Clearly, the social care role is frequently one of mediation and assessment, involving a need for knowledge both of social policy and of the resources available. The importance of social context is apparent in all the examples, and the service users involved are, like others in need of social care, experiencing distress and various forms of actual or potential social exclusion. Some of the themes illustrated above relate directly to key values of respect, or empowerment. There can be no question that social work and social care have much to offer in situations such as those described.

Confidence about the nature of our contribution is a keystone for successful interdisciplinary working. Social care with dying people inevitably involves co-operation across boundaries of health and social care. Specialist services for children and adults demonstrate that service users need help from people who are prepared to work together in their interests. For social care workers, the current climate is not one in which it is easy to gain credibility with colleagues from health services. This has to be done on an individual basis. The example of specialist services teaches us that credibility is gained on the basis of demonstrated commitment to the needs of the service user, and confidence about our own contribution to care. This can mean emphasising the distinctive nature of what we can offer, whilst not being 'precious' about professional boundaries. There are genuine differences of approach and of culture within health and social care. These may need to be addressed. This is not easy at a time when many in social care themselves feel critical of the directions being taken and undermined from within as well as from outside. Nevertheless, examples of good practice can be found in mainstream and specialist services; we need to build upon these.

5.3   Issues of Training and Support

Most of the practitioners I have asked did not feel that working with people who were dying was essentially different from other areas of social care. In this sense, there were not any training needs that were distinctive or different. The main quality emphasised was an ability to know oneself and to be reflective as a practitioner. In order to do this, and to maintain the ability to reflect on practice experience, regular supervision was essential. There was considerable concern that this, once seen as a benchmark in social care, is being eroded, and this concern is, sadly, supported by reports in the social work press (Thompson 1999).

Anxiety was also expressed about care assistants and their need for support in situations that could be emotionally very difficult, as in the following example.

- A service user with severe MS died in the arms of her long-term care assistant, who received no support from supervisor. In another situation, it was known that a service user's death was likely to be by choking. There was concern for the care assistants who were with her overnight.

A trainer spoke of the enormous reservoir of unresolved grief carried by frontline workers such as home carers or care assistants who may be faced with death unexpectedly. One social worker said that in her view, much depended upon the support given by the care manager to her staff, and this could vary between individuals.

This issue is also reported in an evaluation of staff needs in a hospice for children (Stein and Woolley 1990). The death of a client often has enormous emotional impact for workers. After a difficult death, it is not unusual for workers to become sick or even leave the service if they are unsupported. This is where teamwork has enormous benefits, particularly if the service user was known to all members of the team. Work-based rituals for dealing with grief have benefit for staff as well as for other residents in institutional settings. Again specialist services have led the way in establishing regular memorial opportunities in institutions, to which surviving parents or relatives are invited. For staff, such occasions are very important. Yet workers stressed that issues of loss exist in social care in all settings; it is just that we are not very good at acknowledging and dealing with these in any other areas of work.

For social workers, the standard allocation of time for supervision is, in many places, not sufficient to address emotional needs as well as covering practical matters of managing a caseload. As one worker put it, if you are not properly supervised, it becomes too painful to use yourself and your own experience, so you will not do it. Work can become superficial and defensive. With people who are dying, it is essential, in the eyes of all the people I have spoken with, to be aware of and to use the self. Specialist palliative care services recognise this need for adequate supervision and routinely offer it. In general nursing, there is now interest in clinical supervision and considerable development both in theory and practice (Bishop 1997). This seems to be another area where social work has led the field and is now losing out. In some places (Thompson 1999), there is a policy on supervision and standards that are monitored. In others, there has been a move away from seeing emotional support as an essential ingredient in social work supervision. A number of people also emphasised the need for reference to be made to issues of training and support in service specifications where services are provided by agencies outside the local authority.

Most workers pointed to particular training courses that had helped them in this work. Some had developed an interest through courses offered outside their work, by specialist organisations such as CRUSE Bereavement Care. Others had attended in-house training. Most felt that the basic knowledge was the same as that needed in all social care – aspects of psychology and sociology and of social policy. Some said that courses were available but that, again, this was a matter of how far a manager was prepared to point these out or support one's attendance on them. There was concern that with a move to more continuing care in the community, home carers would increasingly be working with and supporting dying people (Sheldon 1998). They need adequate training and support for this role.

As some aspects of the purchasing function of social work emphasise practical response at the expense of emotional involvement, there was a suggestion that it would be frustration rather than emotional overload that caused stress for social workers. This frustration could arise from the inability to commission adequate services, in the view of one very experienced worker. Here again there is clearly a tension. A study in the USA found similar difficulties and frustrations for social workers to those experienced currently in the UK, including expectations of 'workers to focus their efforts more narrowly on efficient discharge plans' (Davidson and Foster 1995). This study suggested management strategies to reduce the strains involved. Team work, peer support and supervision are elements in this and other studies that have looked at issues of burn-out in this area of work.

5.4 Conclusion: Social Care with People who are Dying

This chapter has illustrated ways in which social care workers from both specialist and mainstream services are working with people who are facing death. Five strands have been identified in their accounts of their work, and these can be seen to relate closely to basic aspects of the social care role. These are not particular to work with dying people, nor are they the 'exclusive' property of social care, although the combination of emotional and practical help, facilitating communication with others in the person's social network and advocating for the service user are perhaps most characteristic. Work with dying people is often carried out in health settings, or with health care colleagues. The social carer in this position needs to be comfortable with working in an interdisciplinary way, and extra training, preferably with health colleagues, may facilitate this. The importance of regular supervision in this, as in all areas of social care, cannot be overemphasised, as a basic precondition for effective work at all levels.

In Chapter 4, the experiences of some service users were presented in terms of 'managing the present', abandoning the future' and issues to do with social connectedness. This may offer a useful framework within which to consider the social care contribution. The practical aspects of the social care role mean that much work is directed towards helping people to manage in the present. Social relations are also a focus for much of social care. Supporting and enhancing social connections and offering help in managing the present do not rest upon awareness of a terminal state. They are as relevant to older people who are not in the 'aware dying role' as to cancer patients who are, and they are just as important as the issue of abandoning the future. There is an argument for suggesting that the emotional work involved in facing one's own imminent death is essentially very lonely and private work. Family, friends and even professional helpers may offer companionship, but often even the closest can offer little more. The issue of social death is perhaps most relevant in looking at the experiences of older people; here the role of supporting and enhancing social connections may be crucial.

It is a great pity if social care workers underrate or devalue the contribution that they can make to the interdisciplinary work of caring for dying people by basing their understanding of their own role upon a theoretical basis that is too narrow. Important as it is to understand the emotional reactions that are likely to occur when people face a diagnosis of terminal illness, our role is broader than this. In order to do the necessary work of grieving, people need help and support in other areas of their life. As current practice demonstrates, it is possible, even within the changing landscape of social care, for both mainstream and specialist workers to offer such help together with colleagues from other disciplines.

6

Understanding Grief and Bereavement

In the overall title of this book, the term 'grief' refers both to the experience of a person facing their own death and to the experience of those who survive the death of another. Some authors (e.g. Seale 1998) suggest that the process is essentially the same, an argument that is outlined below. In line with the dominant trend in the literature (Cowles and Rodgers 1993), however, grief is linked here – and in the overall structure of this book – with bereavement, and thus with the experience of those who survive the death of another person.

This chapter looks at a variety of definitions of key terms, as well as offering an overview of theoretical understandings and models relating to grief and bereavement. Matters of definition introduce us to areas of key theoretical debate. Is grieving an emotional or a cognitive process, for example? Is it an instinctive and universal human response or one that is subject to cultural variation not only in its expression, but in terms of experience also? Following a period of relative stability in relation to theoretical understandings, the late 1990s has been called a 'revolutionary' time (Walter 1997b: 173). New models of grieving have been proposed by Stroebe and Schut (1995, 1998, 1999) and Walter (1996), representing on the one hand a psychological approach and on the other a sociological one. The reactions of specialist social workers to these understandings is positive, reflecting a view that close links can be made with their practice.

This chapter outlines both the newer theories and some more familiar precursors, and also gives suggestions, based upon case examples from a wide range of social care settings, of how the recent theories might relate to various areas of practice. Finally, I shall look at what is distinctive about a child's experience of grief and at what is known of the longer-term consequences of what has been termed 'unresolved grief'.

6.1 Defining Key Terms

What is **bereavement**? Stroebe and Schut state that

> Bereavement is the situation of a person who has recently experienced the loss of someone significant through that person's death. (Stroebe and Schut 1998: 7)

Grief is not so easy to define. Indeed, the definition of grief and grieving reflects core issues in theoretical understandings of the concept. It is important therefore to look at a number of definitions and note their different emphases. Thus, Marris speaks of grieving as

> ... the psychological process of adjustment to loss. (Marris 1986: 4)

Fahlberg (1991) suggests that

> Grief is the process through which one passes in order to recover from a loss. (Fahlberg 1991: 141, cited in Howe 1995: 58)

Parkes (1996) has the following:

> Grief is a process, not a state.... It is the reaction to loss, usually of a person. (Parkes 1996: 7)

Even in these three, very similar, definitions we see some variation. All emphasise process, and that this can relate to loss in a general sense (not only death), but one mentions recovery, whilst another speaks of adjustment. These two words reflect more than one theoretical debate. To what extent should grief be considered to be like an illness, and does one 'recover' from serious loss or, as many might say, to what extent do you or should you expect to 'get over it'? Many bereaved people argue that this is neither possible nor desirable.

Another theoretical discussion concerns whether grief is in the heart or the mind. On the one hand, grief is often seen as an emotional process, as in the following definition:

> Grief is the primarily emotional reaction to the loss of a loved one through death, which incorporates diverse psychological and physical symptoms and is sometimes associated with detrimental health consequences. (Stroebe and Schut 1998: 7)

Other authors (e.g. Walter 1996) have stressed its cognitive aspects. For example, Klass, Silverman and Nickman (1996) refer to grief as being about

> ...construction and reconstruction of a world and of our relationships with significant others. (1996: 20)

This idea is more in line with the theoretical underpinning of Seale's work, referred to in Chapter 3 (sections 3.4 and 3.8). The two most recent theoretical models – those of Stroebe and Schut (1999) and of Walter (1996) – reflect these two different emphases. One is a psychological approach – albeit with acknowledgement of the social context – the other a sociological model which stresses the need for the bereaved to reconstruct their sense of self and of the social world.

Mourning is not the same as grief, although associated with it. Turning again to Stroebe and Schut, we see that

> Mourning refers to the social expressions or acts expressive of grief, which are shaped by the practices of a given society or cultural group. (Stroebe and Schut 1998: 7)

There is an important distinction here. Whilst bereavement and grieving are often seen as individual states or processes, albeit socially shaped (or, for sociologists, essentially socially constructed), mourning is a term which refers to shared, socially prescribed practices. Oliviere and his colleagues neatly summarise the differences between these three concepts, as follows:

> Bereavement is an event; grief is the emotional process, mourning is the cultural process. (Oliviere *et al.* 1998: 121)

The authors go on to amplify this, but as Walter (1999) notes, most Western texts make such distinctions, the consequence of which is that culture can be seen to influence mourning, but not grief – a point that he rightly disputes.

Bereavement and these associated processes are, then, usually considered to be matters concerning the survivors: those who are left after the death of a significant other. In contrast, Seale (1998) suggests that separation of the emotions experienced by the dying person and those of the bereaved is unhelpful. This is for two reasons. Firstly, he sees grief as follows:

> the phenomenon conventionally referred to as 'grief' is in fact an extreme version of an everyday experience of 'grief' which is routinely worked upon in order to turn the psyche away from awareness of mortality and towards continuation in life. (Seale 1998: 211)

In this analysis, therefore, there is no necessary connection with an actual death, and certainly no distinction to be made between 'before' and 'after' the event. Secondly, he argues that within the revivalist discourse (section 3.4 above), the aware dying person actually becomes the main mourner for his or her own death. Seale points to the similarities between the emotional stages proposed as typical in the grief of the bereaved (below, section 6.2.1) and those which are characteristic of dying persons (above, section 3.9) to argue that this process of grieving is fundamentally the same process. Notwithstanding the attractions of this argument, the distinction between dying and bereavement is retained here.

A concept that does relate to this debate is, however, the idea of anticipatory grief. Like the concept of grief in the majority of the literature, this refers to the emotions of survivors, not of the dying person. The term was used initially by Lindemann (1944) in relation to the responses of women who anticipated the death of their husbands in the Second World War. The argument is that expectation of death can initiate a process of grieving essentially similar to that following a death. This is seen to be helpful in terms of later grieving insofar as much of the 'grief work' (see below) has already been done, particularly if the period of absence or 'dying' is a long one. Various studies have looked at whether this seems to occur in other death-related situations, and results are contradictory, due, suggests Evans (1994), to conceptual confusion. She follows Aldrich (1974) who has outlined important differences between the emotional reactions of relatives prior to a death and those after it. She argues that the grief before death is a reaction to other losses that the illness brings, suggesting that it would be better to use the term 'terminal response' rather than 'anticipatory grief' for this. In cases such as Alzheimer's disease, where the dying person is seen by carers to be socially dead before clinical death occurs (see Sweeting and Gilhooly 1997; and above, section 3.2), we may think of this pre-death grieving not as anticipatory grief but as grief in response to the social death that has already occurred. There is theoretical debate, then, as to whether the distress that relatives and friends may feel prior to a person's death can, or should, be understood as the start of the process of grieving that continues after death.

6.2   The Grieving Process and the Grief Work Hypothesis

Like social work, the study of grief and grieving has roots both in psycho-analysis and in the social sciences. Following initial work by Freud in 1917 (Freud 1957), Bowlby (1969, 1973 and 1980) later made a distinctive but central contribution through his studies of young children and the effects of maternal deprivation, and the development of Attachment Theory. This has formed the theoretical basis of much subsequent work, including that of Parkes (1970, 1996), who remains a leading writer and practitioner in this field. One of Parkes's early studies (of the first year of bereavement) was carried out together with social scientists Glick and Weiss (1974). Earlier, Marris (1958), also a sociologist, had introduced a number of key concepts following a study of widows in London. Marris has since argued (1991) that attachment theory offers a way of bringing together the disciplines of psychology and sociology. Howe (1995) points to the importance of attachment theory for social work practice.There are links too between the contemporary sociological ideas of Giddens (1991) and the earlier work of Donald Winnicott – like Bowlby, a psycho-analyst. Giddens's recent writings form a reference point for the sociology of Seale (1998) and Walter (1994, 1996, 1999), both of whom are currently involved in the development of sociological understandings of grief and bereavement.

Interest in grief and the grieving process has, in large part, been driven by a focus upon practice, led until recently mainly by psychiatrists such as Colin Murray Parkes, from the UK, and Beverley Raphael (1984), from Australia. In the USA, leading researchers include William Worden, who is a Professor of Psychology, and Phyllis Silverman, who has a social work background. In this sense, it falls firmly within 'patient-centred medicine' dominated by the 'psi-sciences' which Seale and others have identified as a characteristic discourse of late modernity (1998: 92 ff). Social care work can also be seen to be part of this broad movement, in which there is a strong emphasis on self-knowledge and reflexive monitoring, as well as being, with its strong state involvement, part of the broader project of modernity (Dominelli 1997: 7). We should not be surprised, therefore, to find strong links between the theory base of social work generally and the classic understandings of grief and grieving.

The account that follows is necessarily selective. There are two parts. Firstly, I focus upon attachment theory, the phases of normal grieving identified by Bowlby (1969, 1973, 1980), and the work of Parkes (1970, 1996), Marris (1986, 1991) and Worden (1991). I then draw out some key themes and issues and outline what has been called the 'grief work hypothesis' (Stroebe 1992). The following section will look at the models proposed by Stroebe and Schut (1999) and Walter (1996 and 1999), considering the extent to which they address some of the issues unresolved in prior theories, and also illustrating their potential as a means of illuminating practice concerns in social care.

6.2.1 Attachment and Loss: Phases, Stages and Tasks of Grieving

Drawing upon studies of infants separated from their mothers, and also work on the behaviour of animals in infancy, Bowlby's distinctive contribution within a psychoanalytic tradition was to see attachment behaviour as instinctive, distinct from feeding and sexual behaviour, but as important. Attachment behaviour is defined thus:

> Attachment behaviour is conceived as any form of behaviour that results in a person attaining or retaining proximity to some other differentiated and preferred individual. (Bowlby 1971: 39)

In healthy development, attachment behaviour leads to the development of bonds, and both the bonds and the behaviour are present throughout the life cycle. The formation, disruption and maintenance of attachment bonds gives rise throughout life to the most intense emotions. Bowlby insisted that this behaviour is in itself normal, and not pathological. Disturbed patterns arise when early attachment experiences follow a deviant pathway. Patterns of attachment are established through experiences of early attachment, and then these characteristic ways of forming social bonds persist throughout life. Howe's book (1995) is a useful source of further detail for the practitioner. Weiss (1991) summarises key features of attachment bonds, and looks at the question of whether adult attachments are developments of the same emotional system, concluding that they are.

Loss of the attachment figure leads to grief, and the phases of normal grieving described by Bowlby (1971) are rooted in his theory of attachment. They are as follows:

- *Shock and denial*, generally lasting a number of weeks;
- *Yearning and protest*, also lasting a number of weeks;
- *Despair*, which may be accompanied by somatic and emotional upset and social withdrawal, and last several months, or even years;
- *Gradual recovery*, marked by increasing wellbeing and acceptance of the loss.

As Parkes (1987: 80) describes, the early stages of acute grief, with associated pining and urge to search for the one who has gone, are, in this
framework, a frustrated form of the separation protest and proximity
seeking of attachment behaviour. This urge to search conflicts with the
awareness of the older child or adult that such search is useless. There
is a tendency therefore to avoid reminders of loss alongside the urgent
pining and yearning. As attachment behaviour is extinguished, there
comes a realisation that 'their basic assumptions about themselves and
about the world will have to change' (Parkes 1987: 80), and this leads to
a time of withdrawal for many people while their world is reassessed. In
this account we see both an instinctive emotional phase which focuses
on the loss, and a more cognitive phase in which avoidance and social
withdrawal are characteristic.

Parkes himself has written widely on the topic of attachment and
bereavement (Parkes 1970, 1996; Parkes and Stevenson-Hinde 1982;
Parkes, Stevenson-Hinde and Marris 1991; Parkes, Laungani and
Young 1997), developing and refining many aspects of theory. Through
his own practice and teaching, and through links with hospices in
London, and his association with organisations for the care of bereaved
people (such as CRUSE Bereavement Care), he has exerted a wide-
spread influence upon the development of both practice and theory.
One important concept that he introduced is that of 'psycho-social
transitions'. Although attachment theory may be seen to provide a basis
for understanding loss and grieving, it is clear that we grieve relationships other than primary attachments. What, Parkes asks, makes some
losses particularly difficult? His answer links to that period of reassess-
ment which follows the initial (and in terms of attachment theory,
instinctually based) searching and pining reaction. Some losses bring
about profound changes to the social environment of the individual.
These he calls 'psycho-social transitions'.

Psycho-social transitions:
- Require people to undertake a major revision of their assumptions
  of the world;
- Are lasting in their implications rather than transient;
- Take place over a relatively short time, so there is little opportunity
  for preparation. (Parkes 1993)

Parkes has done much work on the factors that predispose people to
a healthy or successful resolution of grief; amongst which preparation
for the loss is important, as is support from others. He calls the sets of

expectations that we have about the world and about how we relate to it, our inner 'assumptive worlds'. This is very similar to Giddens's practical level of consciousness, already described above (section 3.4). Both authors agree that this is the basis for a feeling of safety and security.

The idea of psycho-social transitions relates closely to work by Peter Marris (1986). Marris studied positive change and innovation and its effects, including research into urban renewal and social change in Nigeria, as well as widowhood. His understanding is also linked to theories of attachment and the ways in which the infant learns very early to balance compliance and protest as strategies for achieving both security and control (1986: viii, and 1991). Three concepts are central in his work:

- *The Conservative Impulse*: 'The impulse to defend the predictability of life is a fundamental and universal principle of human psychology. Conservatism in this sense is an aspect of our ability to survive any situation; for without continuity we cannot interpret what events mean to us, nor explore new kinds of experience with confidence' (Marris 1986: 2).
- *Structures of Meaning*: 'The organised structures of understanding and emotional attachments by which grown people interpret and assimilate their environment' (Marris 1986: 4).
- *Grieving*: 'The psychological process of adjusting to loss' (Marris 1986: 4) – we feel bereft not only of what is lost but also of part of our understanding of the environment.

The structures of meaning described by Marris seem to be another way of describing the 'assumptive worlds' of Parkes, and again bear a close relation to Giddens's practical level of consciousness, which includes everyday habits and routines and taken-for-granted assumptions about the world. Such concepts explain the enormous upheaval that is involved in any loss that forces us to re-examine everyday habits and assumptions. This upheaval is well expressed by Marris when he says that

> Losing someone you love is less like losing a very valuable and irreplaceable possession than like finding the law of gravity to be invalid. (Marris 1982)

Last of the authors to be considered in this section is William Worden (1983, substantially revised 1991). The title of his book reveals his orientation towards practice: it is called *Grief Counselling and Grief*

Therapy and sub-titled 'A handbook for the mental health practitioner'. Worden's work is rooted within attachment theory, but he sees the idea of phases or stages of grieving as too passive and deterministic, proposing instead four 'tasks' for the bereaved person to accomplish. His justification for introducing the concept of 'Tasks of Mourning' is that they are 'much more consonant with Freud's concept of grief work and imply that the mourner needs to take action and can do something' (Worden 1991: 35). The tasks are as follows:

- *Task I*   To accept the reality of the loss;
- *Task II*   To work through to the pain of grief;
- *Task III* To adjust to an environment in which the deceased is missing;
- *Task IV*   To emotionally relocate the deceased and move on with life. (Worden 1991: 10–17)

Worden's formulation of Parkes's determinants of grief has also been found useful as a checklist for practice. These are:

- Who the person was
- The nature of the attachment
- Mode of death
- Historical antecedents
- Personality variables
- Social variables

Changes made to Worden's formulation between the first and second edition of his work include an alteration to the fourth of his tasks, from 'withdrawing emotional energy from the deceased and reinvesting it in another relationship' to that shown in the list above. This change is significant. Other writers and researchers have questioned the idea of emotional withdrawal, as we shall see, and this has been one factor leading to alternative models being put forward.

6.2.2   Themes and Issues: Challenge to the Grief Work Hypothesis

Movement for change has come from two principle sources: firstly, from the views of some groups of service users who have found that these models did not always do justice to their experience (Klass, Silverman and Nickman 1996; Walter 1996); secondly, from research that increasingly points to the importance of cultural and gender differences in grieving, for which established models make no space (Stroebe 1998; Stroebe and Schut 1998, 1999).

Whilst gender differences in grieving patterns have been noted for some time they have not until recently been seen as a challenge to established models (Klass, Silverman and Nickman 1996; Seale 1998). Although (unusually) female perspectives on grieving have been theoretically dominant (Stroebe and Schut 1999; Walter 1999), specific attention has been paid to men's experiences of grief by Lister (1991), Staudacher (1991), Thompson (1997b) and Williams (in Oliviere *et al.* 1998) each of whom do so from a concern to develop practice. Stroebe (1998) also offers a useful review of gender differences in the context of arguing that her new framework or model, considered in detail below, is one that can take account of such difference.

Theories that ignore differences in culture can easily become the basis for practice that is unconsciously racist. Gunaratnam (1997) argues that this occurs in relation to interventions with some groups of dying and bereaved people in Britain, where interest in religious and cultural differences amongst minority ethnic groups has reinforced rather than challenged notions of professional dominance (see also Currer 2000). Rosenblatt puts the position as follows:

> New anthropological studies of dying, death and grief suggest that there is no one grief theory or one psychology of ego defences that applies to everyone...Western cultural concepts such as 'dying' and 'grief' originated in the context of its culture. It now seems that realities differ so greatly from culture to culture that it is misleading and ethnocentric to assume that Western concepts apply generally. (Rosenblatt 1993: 13)

We look below at the ways in which Stroebe and Schut's recent model (1999) seeks to make room for differences of gender and culture.

Concern has also been expressed by black social workers (Gambe *et al.* 1992) about some aspects of attachment theory which, as we have seen, forms a basis for much of the theoretical work in relation to loss and grief. These authors argue that whilst attachment theory is an important basis for childcare practice, it can incorporate a Eurocentric view of child rearing. When certain culturally variable practices become seen as superior and universal, theory becomes ethnocentric and practice which is based on such theory can be unconsciously racist. Feminist writers have also expressed concerns about some aspects of early attachment theory.

One concept that has run through much of the work on grieving is what has been called the 'grief work hypothesis' (Stroebe and Stroebe 1991; Stroebe 1992). It is argued that, central to theories about 'recovery' from bereavement has been a hypothesis which has rarely been questioned. This is defined thus:

> the concept of grief work implies a cognitive process of confronting the reality of loss, of going over events that occurred before and at the time of death, and of focussing on memories and working towards detachment from the deceased. (Stroebe and Stroebe 1991: 479)

This hypothesis is traced in theories from Freud onwards. Based upon research evidence, in which gender (Stroebe and Stroebe 1991) and culture (Stroebe 1992) are central issues, the authors suggest that grief work is not always essential for adjustment to bereavement, and also that it is not a universal concept. An alternative, narrower definition is offered as follows:

> grief work is a cognitive process involving confrontation with and restructuring of thoughts about the deceased, the loss experience, and the changed world within which the bereaved must now live. (Stroebe 1992: 33)

As already noted in relation to changes made by Worden (1991), a major difference lies in the increasing realisation, strongly stated by Wortman and Silver (1989), that detachment is not the goal of all bereaved people, and continuing involvement with the deceased person may not be a sign of pathology. Use of the word 'pathology' is itself an indication of the preoccupation, in much of the literature, with identification of patterns of 'abnormal grief'. Stroebe and Schut (1998) summarise this concept as follows:

> Pathological grief is a deviation from the norm (i.e. the grieving reaction that could be expected, given the extremity of the particular bereavement event) in the time span, or in the intensity of specific or general symptoms of grief. Subtypes have been identified as chronic, delayed or absent grief. (Stroebe and Schut 1998: 9)

Such conceptions reflect the medical nature of many of the theories about grief (Stroebe and Schut 1999: 203), and can be viewed, in sociological terms, as an aspect of the way in which 'grief experts' may regulate the grieving process in our society (Walter 1999). Identification of those who are 'at risk' in some way is, however, an aspect of most practice intervention, and appears in more refined guise in later formulations, as we shall see. Whilst the sociologist can stand apart from such judgement, the practitioner cannot, although it is to be hoped that it is the service user, rather than the practitioner, who defines distress or 'pathology' in the context of their own life.

6.3 Theoretical Developments and Debate

Although rooted in practice concerns, and forming the basis of bereavement counselling (often in the voluntary sector), classic understandings of grieving have not fitted entirely comfortably within mainstream social care, since their focus has been weighted towards the individual – leading to an emphasis upon the need for one-to-one counselling. With this, there has been some tendency to neglect aspects of the social context so central to the social care role. The more recent contributions of Stroebe and Schut (1999) and of Walter (1996, 1999), which are considered next, have much to offer both the specialist and the mainstream social care practitioner. These authors pay attention to issues of social connectedness. The next section outlines these models, and gives some suggestions of how they may relate to practice scenarios in social care.

6.3.1   The Dual Process Model of Coping with Loss

Stroebe and Schut have put forward a model of grieving (1995, 1998, 1999) that identifies two categories of stressor in bereavement. The bereaved person has to cope both with the loss experience itself, and with other changes and adjustments that result from it. This leads to two orientations, which they describe as 'loss orientation' and 'restoration orientation'. Both are aspects of the way in which the survivor assimilates the enormous change in their life following a major loss. Both involve both negative and positive emotions. In loss orientation, the grieving person will focus upon what has gone and remember the past. This encompasses the 'grief work' of previous theories. It will involve remembering, and yearning, with negative feelings predominating at first, but maybe also some enjoyment of good memories, particularly as time passes. 'Restoration' orientation also involves both positive and negative emotions as the bereaved person faces new challenges and tasks resulting from the death. Its focus is the present and the future rather than the past, but there is no suggestion here of a progression or staged model.

Fundamental to the model is the notion that there is *oscillation* between coping with these two dimensions of the loss experience, as well as movement between confronting these stressors and avoiding them altogether, perhaps by concentrating on something else. Complicated or pathological grief is seen as involving 'disturbances of oscillation' (Stroebe and Schut 1999: 217). Examples might be a grieving person who focuses upon the loss to the exclusion either of taking time out from grief, or of paying attention to the (often more practical) changes that need attention. Alternatively, another person may not seem to focus at all upon the loss, but appears to 'carry on as normal'. Stroebe and Schut (1999: 215) explain how this model links with others in the field of psychology, and in the study of grieving, particularly noting how Worden's task model might be amplified to take account of both orientations.

One of the distinctive features of this model of grieving is that it takes explicit account of gender and cultural differences (Stroebe and Schut 1998, 1999). In terms of gender, there is a suggestion that women are more oriented to loss, and men to restoration, but that both aspects are necessary for adjustment. This can have particular consequences for parents who have lost a child, since different coping styles may lead to misunderstandings in their relationship. In relation to culture, it is suggested that different cultures may specify that one or other orientation is more acceptable or appropriate. Thus we find that in certain societies, the bereaved person is expected to move on very quickly from expressing distress; in others, this may be prescribed for much longer. One of the most striking reports of research is Wikan's study (1988) of two Muslim societies in which the correct behaviour for those who are bereaved is totally different. She describes how in Bali, there is an apparent absence of emotion, a lack of crying and presentation of a smiling face by survivors following a death, whilst in Egypt, extensive and prolonged crying is encouraged. In Britain, cultural norms are no longer as explicit as they were in previous centuries when formal periods of mourning were marked by changes in expected dress and behaviour. Nevertheless, loss orientation is expected in early bereavement, and viewed with sympathy by others, but this sympathy evaporates at a certain (unspecified) date when the person is expected to be 'getting over it'. This fits with Walter's proposal (1999) that societies and families offer various socially approved 'scripts' for grieving.

As we have seen, the notion of 'taking time off' from grieving is integral to the model. Stroebe and Schut argue that there is a continuum between approach and avoidance, and that at times an individual may avoid their grief in a way that is not denying it. We have already seen in the discussion of Parkes's work above that earlier work did include the idea that individuals avoid their grief as well as focussing upon it. In my experience, children and adolescents seem more accepting of this kind of 'time out' from intense emotional trauma; I have often seen adults upset by the ability of children to apparently 'switch off' and be distracted from grief by other activities. Adults may interpret this as 'not caring'.

■ A girl of 15 who was seeing a bereavement counsellor some months after the death of her father reported how she had wanted to go to her weekly gym class in the week leading up to the funeral. Her grandparents who were staying in the house were horrified, and forbade her to do so, chastising her for her lack of feeling. She said that she had been devastated by her father's death, but needed to be out of the atmosphere in the house for a while and able to talk with her own friends about other things. She was very hurt that people thought she didn't care.

In Stroebe and Schut's model it is a legitimate aspect of grieving to take 'time out'.

In a number of ways, then, the Dual Process Model of grieving seems to be useful for social care practitioners. Firstly, it does address issues of culture and gender in ways that seem to offer a satisfactory basis for practice that is anti-oppressive. Secondly, it seems to offer a way of understanding the dual concern that I have already pointed to as distinctive of social care. Social care workers spend much of their time helping people with practical matters. They are not counsellors with a focus exclusively upon emotional issues. The inclusion in the Dual Process Model of 'restoration', which can include practicalities and attention to current circumstances and changes, would seem to fit well with this role. It also fits well with a focus on empowerment, which is a key social work value.

Speaking on the basis of practice experience, students have given examples of the dual orientation in a wide variety of death-related situations, as well, interestingly, as in some which have not involved death, such as moving to residential care or the loss involved in adjusting to disability, for example. In relation to bereavement, they have observed oscillation between loss and restoration orientation in the case of an older woman with learning disabilities whose long-term companion had died, as well as in a 5-year-old child, following his mother's death. In some instances, however, there has been preoccupation with loss to the exclusion of restoration orientation. For example, a 90-year-old woman made no move to adjust to a move to residential care on the death of her partner; earlier in life her children had all died, and she saw nothing but loss in the present.

Application to practice situations can yield fresh insights. Focus upon restoration usually entails learning new skills or involvement in changed ways of interacting with others. It is clear that for those who are subject to discrimination, such attempts can be thwarted in ways that enhance the loss. The example was given of a Filipino woman who moved to sheltered housing on her husband's death, only to meet with racial hostility from other residents, which reinforced for her the loss of her husband, as he had protected her from such abuse. Further examples given by students have related to situations of discrimination on the basis of disability or sexual orientation.

Stroebe and Schut (1999) make it clear that 'restoration' is not used within the model as an outcome, but for the series of stressors or challenges that accompany loss of a particular person and that therefore also demand attention after a death. Examples have been given above both of situations where individuals seem themselves to choose not to engage with this aspect of grief, and where they are prevented by others from doing so. The reverse may occur in situations where there is pressure to attend to changed circumstances following a loss, at the expense of giving time and attention to focussing on the primary loss itself. This is the situation very often for service users who are required to make quick adjustments to secondary losses (like moving home) and are in a situation (such as some residential care homes) where their loss is not permitted time or space. Oscillation can therefore be disturbed by social as well as psychological processes.

6.3.2   Walter's Contribution

As part of a body of work whose main purpose is to offer a sociological analysis of grieving over time and place (Walter 1994, 1999), Walter has put forward a 'new model of grief' (1996) that pulls together in an accessible manner some of the criticisms of earlier theory. We have already seen that earlier theories of grieving have been based upon what has been termed 'the grief work hypothesis' (Stroebe 1992), in which detachment from the loved one who has died is a goal, and it is the purpose of the grief process to move on. The essence of Walter's (1996) paper is to suggest that the purpose of grief is not detachment but resolution through 'finding an appropriate place' in the lives of the survivors for the person who has died. Whereas previous models have focussed on the internal emotional process, Walter (1996) sees talking with others who have known the dead person as crucial in bereavement. His model is based, like Seale's work (1998), in a sociological tradition led by Giddens (1991), in which creation of a life story, or biography, is an ongoing task throughout life, and grief is the process through which this is completed after death.

Walter's model draws upon research (such as Wortman and Silver 1989; Klass, Silverman and Nickman 1996) which has demonstrated that many bereaved people do not wish to 'let go' of their relationship with the dead person. A continued sense of their presence is common and not seen as pathological. In his later book (1999), Walter identifies the different ways in which societies and individuals integrate the dead into ongoing life. Like Stroebe, Walter acknowledges that this interpretation is not entirely new. He also realises that talking with others who knew the dead person is not possible for many in Western societies which are characterised by geographical mobility and where work and leisure are often separated. Nevertheless, where it is possible, the funeral can be an occasion when people have an opportunity to meet and engage in this process of reassessing the life of the person who has gone. This ritual, when it is personal and meaningful, and letters of condolence, are ways in which the process of 'relocation' of the dead person occurs.

Walter is interested in the role that professionals (and others) play in regulating or 'policing' grief. In his 1996 paper, he suggests that professional helpers are usually 'second best' because what the bereaved person needs to do is to talk with others who knew the deceased. Far from upsetting professionals (Stroebe 1997), this is usually well acknowledged by paid carers, but also raises the familiar question of when (and in what ways) outside intervention can be of particular value. There are occasions when it may be preferable to talk to a stranger. Interestingly, a number of practice examples suggest that the professional may have a role as 'audience'. This would be compatible with the main tenor of the model. In the cases both of a man whose partner had recently died of AIDS and of an older man who had been a popular community figure, the social worker was included by the mourners as one to whom the story could be told afresh, thus being incorporated into the process of biography construction.

My work with bereaved people through CRUSE suggests that in encouraging the story to be told, the counsellor or helper is helping the bereaved person to construct their own story – rather like rehearsing or learning their lines. In Walter's model, the significant others contribute to the story being told, thus helping to construct an accurate and stable shared image. In the counselling situation, the person concerned is straightening out his or her own version. In his later analysis (1999: 124), we find the suggestion that help in bereavement may be sought by individuals either because their grief is 'under-regulated' or as a space because informal helpers seek to impose their expectations (a form of over-regulation). In the first situation, a person may feel they do not know what is expected or normal, and seek reassurance. In the second, their own unconscious expectations and those of others may be conflict- ing or oppressive.

The importance of rituals such as funerals is often underlined when it is not possible for someone to take part. Distance was a factor for one woman whose only son had lived abroad; she was very anxious in her grief to 'reconstruct' details of his life from the accounts of those who had known him. In the Lockerbie plane bombing, it seems that people who were on the spot and who cared for the dead and for their posses- sions became part of the 'story' that relatives needed to hear (*Everyman* TV programme, BBC, 29 November 1998). For a refugee from Bosnia, a return later to bury those he had seen brutally killed was a critical turning point in his own grief, and involved sharing his story with others who had experienced the killings. Workers tell of children who were not included in funeral and other family rituals, whose grief seems to have been blocked. Of course, this model is not the only one to acknow- ledge the critical part that ritual can play. Nor are paid carers strangers to rituals and their significance; it falls to many home carers or residen- tial workers to be the only mourners at the funeral of an aged resident – a sad reflection of the social death that may have occurred many years before. This is a 'final chapter' that tells a story without words.

Walter's work has relevance for social care in many ways that go beyond the applicability of his 'new model'. In broad terms, we are alerted to the existence of a variety of cultural 'scripts' that govern grieving, to questions of how grieving is socially regulated, and why, and the part that we may play in this – either empowering or further oppressing service users. He has comments to make too that are relevant to reminiscence work (1999: 41) – is remembering always a good thing? Interestingly, he also says that 'typically, bereavement agencies help clients manage their emotions, and may be ill-suited to clients whose needs are practical or economic' (1999: xvii). Social care, with its dual focus, may indeed offer a more rounded service than agencies that offer counselling alone. We know from work in the time following a disaster (Newburn 1993; and Chapter 8, below) that both levels of care are important in bereavement.

6.4   A Child's Grief

This area is one of central importance in social care. Within specialist teams, it has often been the social worker who has developed a particular role in work with children (Monroe 1998). Outside palliative care services, work with children and families constitutes a major area of statutory responsibility within social care, and much of this concerns loss, although this is not always death related. In looking at theoretical understandings we need therefore to ask what, if anything, is different about a child's experience of grief. Jewett (1984) describes three phases of grief in children. These are:

- *Phase One: Early Grief*, characterised by shock, denial, disbelief and alarm.
- *Phase Two: Acute Grief*, similar to Bowlby's 'yearning and protest'; searching.
- *Phase Three: Integration*, 'the worst has happened and I have survived'.

Much of the work on grief in children is based in the same theoretical traditions as those already described. There are, however, two key differences to be noted. One of these – the level of cognitive development – is psychological and intrinsic to the child; the other concerns social relations and the relative powerlessness of children. In relation to the first, we know that understanding of the concept of death develops through various stages in line with other aspects of cognitive development. A young child has no awareness of the finality of death, for example, and this is not helped by cartoons in which the central character may be killed and jump up again a minute later. Later, there is a phase of 'magical thinking' when a child believes that they can directly cause events to happen – this clearly makes the regret and guilt which is a part of grief at any age more direct and poignant. Whilst the adult may feel responsible for events leading to a death (for example, if only we had left the house an hour earlier, he would not have been involved in that accident), a child of a certain age may be convinced that they are

directly responsible. The age of the child, and his or her level of cognitive development are therefore critical factors. There are various
excellent source books that go into more detail – Dyregrov (1991) and
Pennells and Smith (1995) are recommended.

Another factor that is critical is the degree of dependence that
children experience. This combines with ideas about the behaviour that
is or is not appropriate for children. Whatever the dominant norms,
children are likely to be more subject than others to someone else's
ideas about what they should or should not do. A practice example will
illustrate this dependence and its consequences.

■   Jane was 11-years-old when she witnessed her father's death
    from a heart attack. Her mother had left them some time earlier.
    She went for help and was subsequently supported, with her older
    brother, by social services in the family home until the day of
    the funeral. After the ceremony, she and her brother were taken
    into care.

In this instance, Jane was helped to remain for a while in the family
home, and supported in attending the funeral, but denied the opportunity to see her father's body, as this was thought inappropriate for a
child, and potentially upsetting. She tried to 'adjust to an environment
in which the deceased is missing' (Worden's Task III, above) by keeping the home tidy and clean, and cooking for her brother, but could not
remain in that home after the funeral. For an older person, the idea of
such a move so soon after bereavement would be discouraged (Help
the Aged 1996). Moreover, her father's culture and beliefs about
appropriate rituals of death were not followed, so these rituals lacked
significance for his children. As a traveller, this man had often talked
with his children about his wish to be cremated with his possessions.
In this instance, protection of Jane and her brother was considered
paramount. As we know, there is frequently a clash between protection
and empowerment. My purpose here is not to criticise the particular
decisions made – although in the case of denying permission to view her
father's body, this was later thought by those concerned to have been
wrong – but to illustrate that, in the case of children, many decisions
are made for them. Social care workers are, of all people, aware of the
ethical and other dilemmas inherent in this.

One of the most systematic recent studies of child bereavement is
the 'Child Bereavement Study' conducted in Boston, USA by William
Worden and his colleagues. Findings are reported in Worden (1996)

and in Klass, Silverman, and Nickman (1996). The study involved 70 families (in which there were 125 children) in which one parent died, together with a matched control group who had not experienced bereavement. The study's authors concluded that the same 4 tasks of mourning applicable to adults are also relevant for children, but 'can only be understood in terms of the cognitive, emotional and social development of the child' (Worden 1996: 12). In addition, Worden and his colleagues have identified 6 factors that influence the mourning process for children who have lost a parent through death. These mediators are:

- The death and the rituals surrounding it
- The relationship of the child with the deceased parent both before the death and afterward
- The functioning of the surviving parent and his or her ability to parent the child
- Family influences such as size, solvency, style of coping, support, and communication, as well as family stressors and changes and disruptions in the child's daily life
- Support from peers and others outside the family
- Characteristics of the child including age, gender, self-perception and understanding of death (Worden 1996: 17)

Worden also reports on how life changed for these children following the death and suggests ways in which we can help bereaved children. He identifies ten needs, as follows:

- Adequate information
- Fears and anxieties addressed
- Reassurance that they are not to blame
- Careful listening
- Validation of individuals' feelings
- Help with overwhelming feelings
- Involvement and inclusion
- Continued routine activities
- Modelled grief behaviours
- Opportunities to remember (Worden 1996: 140f)

Worden argues that children over five-years-old should be given the opportunity to attend the funeral if they wish, but that this choice should be an informed one, and there should be careful preparation before the event. He also discusses other ways in which children can be involved – such as suggesting something that they would like to be buried with the person, maybe a letter or drawing they have made. One way in which children may be excluded is by being denied the opportunity to give as well as receive comfort (see list of needs in leaflet for 'The Candle Project', St Christopher's Hospice 1998). This key dimension is missing in Worden's list.

An increasing number of resources are available for those working with children who are grieving (Smith and Pennells 1995 offers a valuable collection). Hemmings (1995) reviews some of the literature and describes a programme of intervention, and Oliviere *et al.* (1998) also includes descriptions of practice interventions and programmes. Games such as *All About Me* (Hemmings 1991) or *The Grief Game* (Searle and Streng 1996) are available as resources to be used in therapeutic settings. Other resources such as *Memory Store* and *Memory Book* (both Barnardo's) are also available for use in situations where a child can build up a collection of things as a way of remembering their past, whether in situations of death or of other movement, loss or change. Such resources seem to be very much in line with the process of biography construction described by Walter, and it is for this reason that I have suggested that practice has at times been ahead of theory in understanding and responding to people's needs at times of major change.

6.5   Consequences of Grief

From the 1960s onwards, various studies have looked at the longer-term effects of bereavement upon subsequent health, including the chances of a link with early death. Reviewing a number of such studies, Stroebe *et al.* (1993) found that 'the bereaved are indeed at higher risk of dying than non-bereaved persons'. Increased GP consultation rates were reported in Parkes's early work, and he has subsequently reviewed the evidence generally (1996). Stroebe and Stroebe (1987) look at the psychological and physical consequences of partner loss in a comprehensive work.

Particular attention has been paid to the effects of bereavement in childhood, and there is some evidence that 'children who are bereaved early are more likely to develop psychiatric disorders in later childhood' (Black 1998), as well as in later life (Brown and Harris 1978). This link has been questioned by Harrington (1999), although without reference to recent evidence. The Child Bereavement Study already described found that a third of the bereaved children in the study did experience serious emotional or behavioural difficulties at some time in the two years after the death. One of their surprising findings was that for a number there was a delayed effect, with risk of disturbance greater in the second year than the first. The authors have looked in detail at risk factors and predictors of risk. Amongst these, they identify as important preparation for the funeral, fear for the safety of the surviving parent, and wider support for the family (Worden 1996).

The literature on long-term consequences has also been reviewed. Worden argues that research results are not conclusive or consistent, but that 'there is more evidence for depression risk and panic attacks, and less for generalised anxiety disorders, suicide and conduct disorders' (1996: 111). Beliefs about long-term consequences have, however, fuelled service interventions – particularly for bereaved children (Stokes and Crossley 1995; Baulkwill in Oliviere *et al.* 1998: 80f). Those who work with bereaved children are in no doubt that there is sometimes a need for grief to be facilitated (*Lifeline*, Summer 1999), to relieve present, if not future pain (Monroe 1999).

6.6   Conclusion: Understanding Grief

In concluding this overview of theoretical understandings of grief and bereavement, it is worthwhile to highlight two key themes that run through these theoretical accounts. These are the themes of coherence – that which gives life meaning – and control.

The notion of powerlessness was introduced only in discussion of a child's experience of grief, but this is, in fact, a far more fundamental issue. Marris (1991) links grief and the way we manage it to issues of overall control in society, suggesting that people who have little power are more subject to loss than those with more power or resources. The theme of powerlessness is central for Bright (1996), whose book is entitled *Grief and Powerlessness*. In relation to Stroebe and Schut's model, I have argued that those who experience discrimination may find that attention to matters of restoration are blocked. Death threatens our ability to exercise control over life and grief is essentially a state in which people feel themselves to be helpless.

In addition, authors such as Parkes and Marris have pointed to the importance of 'structures of meaning' or of the assumptions we make about the world. Death also threatens meaning; the ways in which we understand life, and the assumptions we have made about it. In a parallel way, depression has been described as characterised by helplessness and hopelessness (Brown and Harris 1978); grief is similarly about both of these. Antonovsky (1987) has identified these two themes of coherence and control as two aspects of the concept of health; little wonder then that they are the aspects of experience which are most threatened by death and the grief which is associated with it. As social care workers, it is often our role to try to help people both to understand what is happening in their lives (the counselling part of the role) and to regain some control over it, maybe through practical means. In understanding grief, it is important that we continue to work at both levels.

7

Experiencing Bereavement

Published autobiographical accounts can be an important source of understanding for the practitioner. Holloway argues that 'these books ...have helped me as a counsellor to understand better what the bereaved are experiencing' (Holloway 1990: 21). Walter comments that he suspects most practitioners like to read such personal accounts more than they like to read textbooks and that 'there is a real sense here in which the expert is learning from the client' (1994: 128).

Such 'learning from the client' fits well with the aims and values of social care. There are a few caveats, however. The attraction of first-hand accounts for the bereaved reader often lies in an explicit appeal to a common basic humanity, to an aim of helping the sufferer to feel that they are not alone (Holloway 1990). Yet they do not (and cannot) reflect universal experiences, but very particular ones that are the product of a social context in which gender and culture are only two important aspects. Walter gives the example of differences between white middle-class culture in which the lack of a male partner might cause social difficulties for a widow, and the custom in some working-class areas where women go out, if at all, with female companions (1994: 127). In many places in the world, social life is predominantly with people of the same gender; the implications of the death of a spouse are then very different from those described by white English widows of a certain age and social class where this is not the case.

Social care seeks not only to appreciate the perspective of service users, but also to acknowledge in a real way that such perspectives differ along the lines of factors such as gender, race, age, ability and sexual orientation. In terms of bereavement, the issue of sexual orientation has at last been acknowledged, and there are now not only accounts of extreme discrimination experienced by gay people following bereavement (Cave 1993), but also accounts of 'good grief' (Cave 1996). In relation to people with a learning disability, their right to grieve is being recognised (Oswin 1990; James 1995), with some services being developed to meet their particular needs (Maliphant 1996). Cultural differences in grieving and mourning tend to be acknowledged through reference to anthropological accounts of widely divergent customs of mourning (Rosenblatt 1993), or descriptions of religious and cultural variations, in terms of public customs and rituals (Firth 1993; Katz 1993; Parkes, Laungani and Young 1997). These focus upon culture rather than race (Gunaratnam 1997) and upon public customs rather than private emotions.

My own experience in Pakistan has left me with two particular memories in relation to bereavement. Firstly, there was the experience (described in the literature concerning customs of mourning: e.g. Jonker 1997) of receiving socially expected visits of condolence from friends and relatives after a death. The second was a memorable incident. This was the sight of a young woman from one of the nomadic Frontier tribes who came every year on foot for her baby to be delivered in hospital. She always brought with her a shoebox, in which to bury the baby. I have no idea of the nature of the medical condition that led, each year, to the death of her child, nor do I know anything about her grief or how to tell of it alongside the written accounts of women in Britain who have experienced stillbirth or miscarriage (such as Kohner 1993; Hayton 1995). Nonetheless, her experience remains with me; an account in pictures, not words. Of course, the differences in this instance were not only of ethnicity and culture but much to do with the level of available services. No account, even of emotional reactions and processes, is or can be free of such contextual matters.

Remembering, then, that autobiographical accounts are not representative, what do they offer the practitioner? First, they broaden experience and extend the understanding born of his or her own situation. Secondly, they can illuminate and bring to life theoretical descriptions and help us to use theoretical understandings more creatively and imaginatively, teaching that no framework can be rigidly applied, for no two accounts are the same. At the extreme, personal accounts (whether written and published or in the form of the life stories of service users) can challenge theoretical understandings, or lead to research that does so. This has been the case in relation to understandings of grieving, where the voices of parents who have lost a child have seemed to be at odds with textbook knowledge (McLaren 1997: 1), leading practitioners and researchers to explore such apparent contradictions (Klass, Silverman and Nickman 1996).

In the rest of this chapter, I will draw upon personal accounts of bereavement, mainly those to be found in the articles and letters published in the journals of the National Association of Bereavement

Services (NABS) and of CRUSE Bereavement Care. These are, then, the experiences of those sections of the British population who are in touch with these particular voluntary organisations and who choose and are able to express their experiences in words. CRUSE is a predominantly white organisation and so is NABS. I include, too, comments from the book by Virginia Ironside (1996), as she draws widely upon first-hand accounts and on her own experience in what she writes, and an example from Maureen Oswin's work (1990), which describes the experience of bereaved people who have a learning disability.

The chapter has three sections. First, I consider individual aspects of the experience of grief, such as physical and emotional processes, the perceived threat to individual survival and questions of movement and change. The focus then moves to social aspects such as feelings of difference and separation from others, and expectations of a return to 'normality' and of reincorporation. There are links here with Walter's work (1999) on regulating or policing grief. Lastly, the question of how we may respond to grief leads to a consideration of who can help and on what basis, and to looking at what these particular grieving people have to say about helpful and unhelpful responses from others.

7.1 Individual Aspects of the Experience of Grief

Not surprisingly, personal accounts by bereaved people offer illustrations of most of the emotional reactions and processes described by psychological theorists. The following are just a selection.

'It is a fact that at the beginning one is numb and acts on auto-pilot. ... The numbness really stayed with me for about two months and I found myself doing things that I can still hardly do now. However, the day came when I literally couldn't get out of bed', writes a widow whose husband died suddenly at the age of 57 (Mrs J. T. 1994). A father writes as follows of his reactions to the death of his 19-year-old son. There was first 'a curious numbness, almost a lack of feeling' which 'did not last long – a few hours at most – and was succeeded by the most overwhelming feeling of grief in which crying and a mind that raced all over the place in confusion seemed characteristic' (Stockwin 1995). A husband wrote after his wife's death from cancer that 'when she died I remember walking down the corridor as if in mid-air. There was no feeling in my body' (Mr G. J. 1996).

'Grief is physical in its manifestation', writes Margaret Nuttall (1994/5) following her husband's decline and eventual death from Alzheimer's disease. Others clearly agree. Mrs J. B. (1994/5) comments on 'the feeling in my stomach of hollowness that no food will satisfy' after the slow death from cancer of her husband at 41. The mother of a 19-year-old killed suddenly in a car crash reports 'a great feeling of fear and dread which was concentrated in the throat and stomach, and a pain in the chest not quite locatable' (Cherry 1993). Even after her sister had been missing for 20 years, Marian Partington (1996) describes the palpitations and nausea that accompanied the wait before being given the news that her sister had been one of the victims of a serial killer. A teenager tells of losing one and a half stone in weight after the death of her father (Shee 1996). Ironside sums up a number of accounts saying that 'all the senses may appear simply to have packed up and said "enough is enough"' (1996: 4).

Guilt is another feature of grief that we find in personal as well as theoretical accounts. It can be of many kinds, as one writer identifies after her husband's death. She says 'I was the one who should have died.' There is also guilt 'about things said and left unsaid (especially near the end) and about the times I'd been impatient and even unkind'. There is guilt 'because I can still enjoy some of the things we used to do together' and 'because I know the end of his story and he had to leave me not knowing what would become of me' (*Chronicle* 1995). Guilt is frequently, Ironside claims, the partner of that powerlessness that defines bereavement. 'On the heels of powerlessness, guilt steps in like a devil disguised as a kindly friend – because the phrase "if only" in itself implies *that something could have been done to prevent it*' (1996: 39, italics in original). Both Bright (1996) and Ironside (1996) particularly emphasise the helplessness and powerlessness of bereavement. This was a theme identified at the end of the last chapter (section 6.6) along with the search for meaning or coherence, which is also apparent in these personal accounts.

Anger has both an individual and a social face. It may seem to arise from the situation itself. This was the case for Mrs J. T., who says nine months after her husband's death, 'I do get angry for him sometimes when I think of all the things we had planned that he won't be able to do, and sometimes angry with him for leaving me like this' (Mrs J. T. 1994). Four months after her father's sudden death from a heart attack, Mrs S. T. writes, 'Today I felt angry . . . I felt angry as I dug the garden, angry that the plants were alive and the planter dead' (Mrs S. T. 1995). It may also arise in relation to the words of others or external events. Thus, a father describes the words of others that provoked 'the first real swell of anger' immediately after his son's accidental death; and others later that 'had the effect of once again touching the anger' (Jenkinson and Bodkin 1996). Mrs Tebbutt's husband killed himself, and she says of the inquest 'I was angry, very angry' (Tebbutt 1994). Again following her husband's suicide, C. reports that her anger was 'incredibly intense' (C. 1996).

Ironside speaks of 'the rage of bereavement', singling this emotion out as underlying the tendency of bereaved people to find fault with almost everything, and the reluctance of others to come near. 'They all come in for flak' she observes (1996: 54), whilst also acknowledging that this rage is likely to be intensified in the case of suicide. 'Unfocussed anger is perhaps the worst to bear because it is so burdensome and unpredictable. It is like heaving around a load of shit encased in an extremely thin bag, one that is liable to split at any time' (p. 56). Rage, she argues, 'is a pretty antisocial emotion at the best of times, even when it is directed against deserving targets' (p. 60). Oswin (1990) tells of a normally placid young man who began to be very angry whilst at the day centre in the months after his father's death. Instead of being seen as a normal reaction to grief, this was interpreted as an aspect of his learning disability.

Misery, depression and despair are described again and again. They may be constant or intermittent, suddenly overwhelming the bereaved, without warning. 'One day you'll be handing over the money in the supermarket queue feeling perfectly fine, and thinking about supper, and the next minute your knees buckle and you're in floods of tears' (Ironside 1996: xviii). These feelings may lessen in time for some, at least in the frequency with which they occur, but some choose to stay with the pain, finding it a link with the one who is lost. Whistler (1987) writes, 'I wanted nothing better than to live always in the immediacy of loss. In the sharpness of it I felt near to her . . . What was unendurable was precisely the idea of "coming through".' Others may wish to leave this misery, but cannot. A state of heightened sensitivity is also described by many, a time when everything feels more 'real' than usual, and this too may be something that is left only with reluctance, despite the pain it has contained.

'The fact of death is extremely difficult to absorb' (Ironside 1996: 10). This is graphically illustrated by Mrs S. T. (1995), four months after her father's sudden death. She writes, 'the first few days I couldn't think of him in the past tense. It was "he likes . . . he says . . .". Then it became "He would like . . ." It must become "He would have liked . . ." It keeps becoming more final. . . . And yet I am so used to his being alive that I have cruel moments of forgetting that he is dead.

Then with a jerk, a sickening thud, the truth hits me again, and again, and again.'

For many people, grief is a threat to survival. A widower comments that 'I did not know whether I would survive, or even wanted to' (Mr G. J. 1996). 'The shock, pain and injustice of the situation you find yourself in leave you feeling that you won't be able to survive', says a widow (*Chronicle* 1994a). Nonetheless, there is also, in most accounts, a sense of movement and change. This woman goes on to say that, later, 'I was able to look back at the black chasm from where I had journeyed and realise that things were improving.... I am not sure about the future, but I am sure that I have one' (*Chronicle* 1994a). Although this sense of movement is apparent in most accounts, it is a matter that is controversial – as cited above, some may not wish to move on. For David, a 14-year-old who has learning difficulties, the pain has a life of its own. Nine months after his father's death, he says that 'the pain attacks me like somebody grabbing me and throwing me down ... Even if a person starts a new life, the pain sits in the corner of their body and can still come out' (David 1999). This links to the theoretical discussion reviewed in the previous chapter (section 6.2.2) concerning working through the tasks of grief. Ironside comments that 'you do not work through grief. It works through you' (p. xvii). It is, for her, passivity and helplessness that are characteristic, and the most difficult aspects of grieving.

7.2   Social Aspects of the Grieving Experience

One striking aspect of accounts of bereavement is the sense of being apart from others or leading life on two levels. The following are some examples. 'You live a double life. You shop, cook, eat, visit friends, entertain, take "holidays" – all without the old joy', says a mother after the death of her 25-year-old daughter (*Chronicle* 1994b). 'It feels as if I am travelling along one road and everyone else is travelling along a parallel road' (Mrs J. B. 1994/5). 'Last evening was so strange. We went to a party – a dozen or so people. None of them knew ... everything was normal, nothing different, nothing unusual. Something in me wanted to shout "But my father died last week. He died. He's dead." I never told anyone all evening' (Mrs S. T. 1995). The sense that life is continuing for others apparently 'as normal' can be an affront to the grieving person, and there is a desire to shatter this illusion. Three days after confirmation of her sister's murder 20 years earlier, Marion Partington recounts how she went to have her hair cut. 'I wanted it shaved off as a gesture to the world that I was grieving, that something huge had happened and that I wasn't the same as I was before it happened' (Partington 1996).

Bereaved people do have a sense of separation and of difference that is reminiscent of some of the anthropological accounts of a 'transitional' or 'liminal' state (above, section 3.5). Yet in our society, this state is no longer outwardly marked by a black armband or other sign. Feeling isolated and lonely is very common, even in the midst of company. Nor are there any rituals of 'reincorporation', or agreed expectations about when the bereaved can be expected to 'be over it'. 'People around bereaved people get impatient far too soon' (Ironside 1996: 80). 'If people expected us to have "got over it" it made us angry. There is no time limit to grieving' (Cherry 1993). The Disasters Working Party (1991) speaks of the painful effect of 'many people's expectation that there should be a "grieve by" date by which time victims should be over their loss'. Many bereaved people speak of the force of social expectations regarding re-entry to 'normal life', but also about the way in which there may be different and even contrary expectations; whatever they do is wrong in the eyes of others.

These observations illustrate well the ways in which grief is socially regulated (Walter 1999) by the self and by others as much as by so-called 'experts'. Different scripts exist that may even conflict with each other. Re-entry into social life is clearly a tricky business, socially monitored, but not socially supported in most instances. Holloway (1990) tells of her client's struggle to explore his own feelings about the right time and way to start going out again after the death of his wife. 'George had grieved for his wife, but was beginning to feel that he would like to make a start in re-integrating himself into the social scene. He was afraid that friends would think that not enough time had elapsed since the death of his wife, and that they would think it "unseemly" for him to be seen enjoying himself.' Sue Stuart (1994) found that 'when I slowly started to enjoy life again and looked happy, it was rumoured that I couldn't be missing Ian all that much, but on the occasions when I was sad and depressed, I was told to stop being so miserable'.

Consideration of social aspects of the experience of loss gives us some clues to responses that might be seen as helpful. Firstly, there is clearly a need for others to recognise and acknowledge the death and the altered state that the bereaved person is in. 'Experience seems to suggest that all that is needed by the bereaved is simple recognition of their loss and their right to grieve' (*Chronicle* 1995). 'I found that the first time I saw someone afterwards, I needed Ian's death to be acknowledged' (Mrs J. T. 1994). This recognition will probably extend to making allowances for changed and unpredictable responses at times. There are also lessons to be learned about sensitivity to issues around emergence from grief and re-establishment of social life. With this in mind, we turn next to consider in more detail the responses that grieving people find helpful, and ask to whom they might turn for help.

7.3   Responding to Grief: The What and Who of Receiving Help

What do those who have been bereaved identify as helpful in those they meet? 'Go on ringing up and visiting in the months that lie ahead. Everyone's life returns to normal, except for the bereaved person's, and in those lonely times it is the continual support that means so much', and 'take food, but also offer to do their washing and ironing' (Mrs J. T. 1994). The cultural context of these accounts is very apparent here. In few other cultures are the bereaved left alone in the early days of grief to do their own cooking or washing. Others endorse this appreciation of practical help. Richard Todd recalls a 'compulsive need to talk to people about the accident and how it was affecting me' as well as a need for company. One of the things that he most appreciated was 'those friends who had open house for me' (Todd 1994). As a young widow, Sue Stuart says that 'one of the first, and very hard, lessons that I learned was not to talk about my situation because it tended to make other people uncomfortable' (1994). This is sad because most writers identify a strong wish to talk about the person who has gone, and some to investigate hitherto unknown aspects of their life and death (Stockwin 1995).

   There are whole lists of remarks or comments that bereaved people have found insensitive or unhelpful, although Ironside does comment that 'what is one person's crass remark is another's words of wisdom' (1996: 120). She suggests that good friends can help simply be being there, by hearing the details over and over; and she also mentions practical help, as many others do. Bereavement, she says, 'is something that has to be endured alone'. Nonetheless, to be abandoned by others in bereavement is not what most seem to want. Help from others who cannot really share the pain may be limited in the comfort it can offer, but its absence is even worse. Who then can offer such help?

Not surprisingly, family and friends are mentioned by many as important comforters. A widow recalls how, after her husband's sudden death 'friends were wonderful, they phoned, wrote and came themselves' and of the 'wonderful supporting cloud of love, support and prayers' (Mrs J. T. 1994). Suri Poulos writes to her dead son of the enormous support of the family's synagogue community after his death in the following words: 'your death helped our synagogue community realise just what a powerful and beneficial force it is' (Poulos 1996–7). Similarly, after the death of his partner, an actor wrote 'Friends were marvellous – the theatrical world has a huge understanding of AIDS and is very supportive. I would spend every Sunday afternoon pouring my heart out to friends over the phone' (G. 1996).

Yet such informal support is not always available, and also has its limitations. Thus, G.'s mother was not amongst his supporters as she did not know of his partner's illness, nor that her son was gay. Others also write of the limitations of even the best of family support. Of her sister, Caroline Saarl writes, 'because of the grief we were all still feeling we were not always what she needed.... It became harder, not easier to talk... She needed to find new friends. People she could confide in, who did not have their own hidden agenda of grief' (Saarl 1997). Many parents bereft of a child point to the fact that 'we're grieving for different people' or 'coping in totally different ways' (both cited in Ironside 1996: 124–5). Jan McLaren, Director of the Laura Centre for bereaved parents, writes, 'At a time when you most need each other for support and understanding, your preoccupation with your own loss may make it difficult for you to help your partner' (McLaren 1995). Ironside (1996: 126) also acknowledges instances where family members did not all feel positive about the person who died, and others where there is competition to be 'chief mourner' or 'most bereft'. Of course it may also be the case that there *are* no family members or friends with whom to grieve; a situation increasingly common for older people and in a highly mobile society (Walter 1996).

In such instances, people look for help beyond those already known to them. Many feel that only those who have had the same experience can understand. In 1994, when she was looking for help for her sister, Caroline Saarl found a complete lack of services for young widowed people. She says 'all I was looking for was an organisation that could put her in touch with other young widowed people. People who would empathise' (Saarl 1997). In 1997, she set up her own (The WAY Foundation), and subsequently received enquiries from over 350 people with the same experience and need for mutual help. Widowed many years earlier at 25-years-old, Sue Stuart had a similar experience of the lack of opportunity to 'share common experiences' (Stuart 1994). As a bereaved parent, Mrs R. writes that 'even the kindest words of friends and counsellors cannot reach the pain inside in the way the sympathy of another bereaved parent can' (Mrs R. 1996). Mr G. J. attributes the welcome at social groups for the bereaved to 'the fact that every person attending has been hurt through loss of a partner, and has felt the loneliness that goes with the loss' (Mr G. J. 1996). The power of shared experience also motivates many who publish personal accounts of grief. Suri Poulos published her *Letters to Gil* – her son who died at the age of three after a car accident – in the hope that others might 'find hope in the future following the death of a loved one' (Poulos 1996–7). And Holloway, reviewing a number of personal accounts, identifies in the accounts she reviews the hope that 'the expression of their own pain and struggle in bereavement might be of some help to others' (1990: 17).

This search for sharing with someone who has experienced the same hurt underpins much service provision. A number of organisations are based upon mutual help, with the helper's personal experience of that particular form of bereavement a key factor. The Compassionate Friends, an organisation for those who have suffered the death of a child, is an example which has formed the basis of research by Riches and Dawson (1997). There is now a tendency for more and more spe-cialisation amongst such groups, as people search for an organisation that has experienced more closely their own grief, so there is increasing fragmentation – subgroups for those bereaved by suicide, for siblings or for young widows, for example. The wish for someone who can share the pain is clearly very strong. Yet Ironside cites a friend who says that 'my own experience would be no help to anyone else if I wrote it, because theirs would be not quite the same' (1996: 167). To what extent can this search for companionship in grief be satisfied? For many, however, mutual help offers both a script and a purpose in grief, as Walter describes (1999: 187f).

For counselling organisations, such as CRUSE, the personal experi-ence of the counsellor is not an issue. Training in the ability to listen to and focus upon the experience of the client is, instead, what is offered. The relationship is deliberately one-way. This is a very different basis for help, which comes closer to that offered by professional carers whose own shared experience is incidental to their role. If such helpers have their own experience of loss, they may not reveal it, recognising that this particular relationship is not a reciprocal one. From comments (albeit published in counselling journals), such help also has its place. A teenager says 'I consider myself to be one of the lucky ones because I was encouraged to see a counsellor' (Shee 1996), and another woman states that 'I was grateful that the counsellor encouraged me to talk... the weekly session was a great relief' (Anonymous 1997). Ironside suggests that 'if your bereavement film gets stuck on constant replay, bereavement counselling can help to jerk you out of either deep depression or obsessive thinking', and that 'children really can benefit from seeing a counsellor who's not involved in any way with the dead person' (1996: 174).

We can identify three categories of persons, then, who offer help in bereavement: firstly, the naturally occurring community of workplace, religious group, family or friends; secondly, the 'community' of fellow sufferers of which one gains membership by virtue of the loss itself; and lastly, there are those who might help precisely because they are 'outsiders' – members of neither of these other communities. In the case of those events known as 'disasters' it was precisely this quality of being 'outside' that made professional social workers of benefit (Newburn 1993), and this can be so in other situations too, offering the person who is bereaved their own space to tell their unique story.

In Chapter 4, which looked at the experiences of those facing their own death, three categories were used to organise these accounts. These were managing the present, abandoning the future, and issues of social connectedness. Managing the present is problematic for many bereaved people also, not because of the extra demands of illness and deteriorating health faced by those who are dying, but because of a sense of unreality and detachment from everyday matters, and waves of powerful emotion. Many cultures do not expect bereaved people to manage the present immediately after a death; mourning rituals are such that others take care of such practicalities. Whereas the dying person has to abandon their future, the bereaved person has to return after a while (perhaps reluctantly) to a future that is irrevocably changed. To some extent, they have to create the terms of that future to include not only the physical absence of the person who has died, but also a renegotiated relationship with them (Walter 1999). Issues of separation and connectedness are crucial. Like the dying person, the bereaved person is both alone and separate in an emotional sense, yet may need companionship and support in re-establishing the terms of social existence. We look in the next chapter at the ways in which social care workers are in contact with bereaved people, and the types of response that services offer.

8

Care Workers' Involvement with Those Who are Bereaved

As we saw in the last chapter, those who are bereaved point to physical and behavioural changes that may be extreme and that can threaten everyday life. In this state of heightened sensitivity and vulnerability, the help and support of others may well be appreciated and needed. Some argue, however, that any professional interest in bereavement is an example of the medicalisation of society that undermines the human capacity to cope with life's difficulties (Illich 1976), whilst others have suggested that some interventions may do 'more harm than good' (Harrington 1999). Help, if needed, should be provided by the informal care networks of friends and family, according to this view.

Arguments for professional involvement on the basis of bereavement alone tend to be based upon concerns about the potential consequences of 'unresolved grief', as discussed above (section 6.5). There is also some limited evidence (Parkes 1980) to suggest that counselling in bereavement is effective for those who perceive their family to be unsupportive, or who are identified as 'at risk'. In consequence, some hospice-based bereavement services adopt a screening procedure based upon vulnerability checklists. 'Support' services will then be offered to a majority (usually by volunteers with a reduced level of training) and 'counselling' to those seen to be at risk of more complicated bereavement reactions (e.g. chapter 6 in Oliviere *et al.* 1998). Bereavement services in these specialist settings are usually offered as an extension of involvement with the family unit at the time of death.

Outside specialist palliative care settings, services specifically for people who are bereaved have not tended to be offered in a routine way by either health or social care agencies. Bereavement services have, at least in the UK, been mainly left to the voluntary sector, where we find both mutual help groups and charities that offer more formal counselling.

The one area in which there has been recognition of the need for a government-funded service for people who are bereaved (as well as for others injured or traumatised) is in response to a 'disaster' (Disasters Working Party 1991; Home Office 1994). Disasters are defined, broadly, as events resulting in actual or threatened injuries or fatalities 'involving large numbers of people, requiring a response that overwhelms the normal resources available' (Cambridgeshire County Council 1998). It is significant that in such instances the government not only recognises a systematic need for psycho-social help, but also sees social care agencies as those with a lead role in providing it (Disasters Working Party 1991). The reason given for a need for this care is the prevention of later, deeper, psychological or social harm and that 'long term and chronic demands on the health and social services may be reduced' (Disasters Working Party 1991: 6). Legal suits for compensation for victims have also played a part in forcing recognition of the need for care – for staff of the emergency and caring professions as well as for those primarily affected.

In disaster work, as in other areas, it is recognised, however, that primary support comes from informal carers and 'that any formal response is intended to complement this primary support' (Disasters Working Party 1991: 3). One argument for a responsibility to intervene comes, in such situations, from the fact that informal care is itself often affected by the scale of a disaster, and therefore the community may itself be temporarily disabled by the event. The same effect is observable within families, where parental grief over the death of a child may leave them temporarily unable to respond to the needs of other children (Dent 1999). In thinking, then, about all bereavement situations, we must ask about the nature and strength of informal community resources and mechanisms. As discussed (section 2.5), these vary between societies, as well as over time.

In many contemporary societies, help is no longer 'naturally' available within local communities, according to some writers (Walter 1996). A decline in religious or other cultural rituals, such as characterises modern industrialised societies, may leave individuals unsupported and without shared ways of managing grief and reducing the chance of negative consequences. Physical mobility may mean that people are scattered and able to offer little in the way of practical help. There is therefore an argument that organisations need to be created (either on a mutual support basis, or more formally through paid workers) to compensate for this cultural vacuum.

The argument that awareness of the needs of grieving people is important for all in social care does not rest, however, on the part that a few may play in specialist or voluntary services with a particular focus upon bereavement. We know from the accounts of bereaved people that inappropriate or insensitive responses to grief (on the part of formal or informal carers) are deeply felt and long remembered. As those paid to offer care to people when they are at their most vulnerable, it is surely the responsibility of social care workers to recognise grief and to respond appropriately to it in the course of work that may have another primary focus. Bereavement has no *necessary* association with health or social care settings, and is in many cases incidental to the service user's involvement with social care. Yet when a service user already in our care suffers a significant loss, care workers need to understand what changes in behaviour and mood to expect, and how to respond. There are also situations in which it is a loss that prompts the referral for help – where the death has removed a main carer upon whom the service user was dependent, for example. In such cases, it is the practical implications of the loss that are often the first reason for contact.

8.1 Bereavement: A Significant Feature in All Areas of Social Care

This section offers examples that demonstrate the varied and extensive ways in which bereavement can be a factor for those working in social care. Children's services are considered first, then those for adults, including, in this instance, services for older people alongside those for adults with a disability, learning difficulty or mental health problem. Services for adults grieving the loss of a child are considered in this section also. Lastly, we will look at specialist services for bereaved children and adults, whether linked to palliative care or, as in many voluntary or community initiatives, set up specifically as a response to bereavement, including loss following large-scale 'disasters'.

8.1.1 Bereavement in Children's Services

Bereavement may, in certain cases, be one of the reasons why a child comes to the notice of the Social Services Department and is defined as 'in need'. In some instances, this may be a need for residential care, and the child will be 'looked after' by the local authority, either in residential setting or by foster parents. Adoption may follow. In other cases, bereavement is not the reason for contact, but a factor in the child's background that has a continuing effect on their behaviour. In others again, a child experiences bereavement during their time 'in care'. This may be the death of a fellow resident, or of a care worker, or of someone in their natural family.

When death of a child's main carer occurs, another must be found. It is not uncommon for a child to have to move school and neighbourhood following bereavement, even if they are to be cared for by familiar adults within the family. Where the care of the child is in question, however, the needs of that child are likely to be assessed by strangers – social workers or those working in family centres – at a time when the child is in the worst throes of grief. They may then have to move to a totally unfamiliar situation. One such instance has already been outlined (Section 6.4, above). Another is given here.

■ Members of Nathan's family were all killed in an accident when he was 6-years-old. He had not been in the car with them but at a friend's house for the day when the accident occurred. A black child from a very religious family, he had no surviving family, and was admitted to a residential care home after the accident, whilst his needs were assessed prior to adoption or fostering in the longer term.

In Stephen's case, there were doubts about the capacity of a surviving parent to care.

■ Stephen was three when he was admitted to a Family Assessment Centre for assessment of his mother's parenting, after the death of his father (who had been his primary carer) and his baby sister whose accidental death he had witnessed.

Alternatively, bereavement may have been a part of the child's recent history, not precipitating a need for care but still a very real and recent memory. This was the case for both Richard and Brian.

■ Richard, a white child aged eight, was in a foster placement. His relationship with his mother was very unstable due largely to her mental health problems and recurrent admissions to psychiatric hospital. Two months before his admission to care, his baby brother had died 24 hours after birth.

■ Brian's father died a year before he came into care at the age of 15. His parents were divorced and the split had not been amicable. His father had been violent towards his mother for as long as Brian could remember. Brian's behaviour towards his mother became increasingly angry and aggressive. He now lived with five others in an adolescent unit.

What of bereavement experienced whilst in care? Like other children, those who are looked after by foster carers or in residential settings experience the deaths of those known to them, whether school friends or family members. For some, members of their natural family will have been exposed to dangers that may be life-threatening, such as substance abuse or mental illness (with the risk of suicide). Such dangers may have been one aspect of their need to be looked after, and it may fall to the social worker to break bad news to the child. Moreover, should there be a death at their school or of someone known to them, children who have a history of loss or of abandonment may be especially vulnerable.

Tragedy can also strike within the residential setting as in any other home.

■ West Lodge is a small group home for eight children between 5 and 16 years. John had been working there five years before being killed in an accident whilst on annual leave. He had been key worker for three of the children and was a popular figure both in the home and in the Department more widely.

In some cases a tragedy will involve illness, natural death or an accident outside the care setting, as in the example above; but it may also be the suicide of a young person or an accident within the care setting that requires investigation. The death of a child 'in care', whether through natural causes, accident, neglect or self-harm, sets off a chain reaction which has repercussions for all in the system, children and carers alike.

This section has concentrated upon bereavement as a factor in the lives of children who are looked after by the local authority, whether in residential or foster care. There are other children, however, who are in receipt of mainstream social work services, and for whom bereavement may be an issue. Any child may be referred (often through their GP or a health route) to a child development centre or for behavioural or psychiatric assessment. School health or welfare services may also be alerted to behavioural difficulties that lead to an assessment of the situation. Social workers are members of such teams, and others may also be called in independently if the child is seen to be at risk or in need as a result of such assessment. Bereavement is one of many factors that can lead to emotional and behavioural difficulties for children (Smith and Pennells 1995; Worden 1996). It is also important to remember that this is an issue for *all* children, including those identified as having learning difficulties, whether in schools for children with special educational needs, in respite facilities or in their own homes.

In considering the effects on a child of the death of someone significant, we need to look too at the needs of children who have a relationship with someone close to death. In statutory services one team leader for a children and families team reports an increase in referrals over the past 10–15 years of children whose parent is terminally ill. This situation may not be one in which the child needs to be accommodated by the local authority (there may be another parent living at home, for example), but is often such that there is a need for practical help, such as childminding. Such referrals are frequently made by health colleagues, or by other family members, such as a grandparent. An extreme example of such a situation arises where a child is the main carer for someone who is seriously ill. Young carers were mentioned in Chapter 2. These are 'children sometimes as young as 8 or 9 who are carrying out the bulk of caring for one or more family members' (Douglas and Philpot 1998: 87). In instances that involve terminal illness and subsequent bereavement, grief is added to the child's practical burdens.

Other children affected by impending death are the siblings of a child with a life-threatening illness. The effects on a child of the death of a sibling (whether following terminal illness or suddenly, after an accident, for example) are considered by Worden (1996) and Dent *et al.* (1996). Local initiatives often involve groups that offer siblings a chance to share their experiences with others similarly affected. In the case of communal tragedy, recognition of the needs of children who are either bereaved or living with traumatised survivors has been shown to be critical (Barnard and Kane 1995, 1996), underlining the similar needs of children caught up in individual family tragedies.

The concern here has been to demonstrate that bereavement is an issue for all working in mainstream children's services. Specialist bereavement services for children will be considered with other specialist services in section 8.1.3, below. Bereaved children are 'in need' of an appropriate response to their grief or bereavement from adults with whom they are in everyday contact. Where those adults are responsible for an assessment of their needs in the context of decisions about placement, it is vital that the effects of their bereavement should be taken into account in any assessment and in care plans made with or for them (Howe 1995). It should also be a focus for direct work, whether as a part of routine care by residential or foster carers, or through referral for specialist help.

8.1.2   Bereavement in Services for Adults

For adults as for children, bereavement may give rise to a referral, or it may occur in the course of contact with those providing services. For service users in long-term contact with services, it is likely that they will experience bereavement whilst in receipt of social care services, particularly in the case of older people. I look first, however, at situations where a death is the reason for service involvement.

In the following situation, a duty social worker from a generic team was faced with death and bereavement when she went out in response to a call from the police to a home where a woman had died suddenly in bed.

■ The worker arrived to find the woman's elderly mother in the kitchen of the house that she had shared with her daughter. She was with a young police officer, who, in his embarrassment, was trying to distract the older woman by talking about football. Although she knew that her daughter had died, the mother had been kept away from her body, which was lying upstairs awaiting the arrival of the coroner's officers. The social worker had been called to make arrangements for the care of the mother, who had no sight and had been totally dependent upon her daughter. The old woman had not spoken since being informed of her daughter's death, and seemed to have little understanding of what was going on around her.

For anyone who is dependent upon another for physical care, whether by reason of age, disability or mental health problems, the sudden death of that carer is likely to lead to a need for assessment of need prior to arrangements for alternative care. In the case of people with a learning disability, loss of a significant person may be followed by loss of home and familiar environment that compounds the grief (Oswin 1990; Atkinson and Williams 1990).

It is quite often the case that an elderly couple may support each other – perhaps having complementary abilities – until the death of one, when the infirmities of the other suddenly seem to be magnified, in part by their grief. In both the following examples, there was a referral to the adult services team for a community care assessment.

■ Florence was 90-years-old. Her three children had all died 50 years earlier. After the sudden death of her husband, she herself had a stroke that led to severe mobility problems. She had no wish to live.

■ Lily had been married for 46 years. Her husband had died unexpectedly after a long illness. He had been well known in the town where they had both lived since childhood.

The death of his wife was the reason for Samuel's need for help at home. In this instance, it is the service provided by the home carer rather than the initial assessment that is illustrated.

■ Samuel had had home care since the death of his wife. He was a white man of 78, who had experienced a number of minor strokes, and now needed a carer to call in three times a day: to get him up, cook his lunch and prepare him for bed. He spent his time watching television and eating sweets. His doctor said that carers should wean him off these, but he was resistant to this. In the two years that one carer had been visiting, he had deteriorated and lost all interest in self-care or conversation. He was not eating or sleeping well, and was very aggressive.

The following referral came from a GP to the community mental health team. Although prompted by bereavement, there was not in this instance an immediate practical reason for social work involvement.

■ June Wright was 72-years-old. She was referred by her GP due to a decline in physical health and suicidal thoughts. She had lived alone for many years and had few friends. It seemed that her only son had lived abroad and had recently died. She had been unable to attend the funeral and constantly referred to her son.

Workers in a hospital setting are also likely to meet with someone's sudden death. The following is a dramatic example of this, again involving the police and a need for investigation.

■ A baby of three months had been brought in dead, suspected of having been killed by his stepfather. The police were involved and waiting to interview the mother and begin an investigation. Nursing and medical staff were all shocked to see the baby dead. The social worker arrived to find a situation characterised by noise, pressure and frantic activity.

In addition to such extreme circumstances, and far more common, are those situations where a baby is stillborn or dies shortly after birth – some 11,000 babies a year in the UK (figure from Thomas 1995; see also Kohner 1993; Fairbairn 1993). Miscarriage is also now recognised to be a source of intense grief for some mothers. Jenny Thomas of the Child Bereavement Trust has explored the feelings of bereaved parents and other family members (Thomas 1995). Grief for a stillborn baby shares some of the features of the death of an older child, but is, in other ways, quite different. Paradoxically, the lack of memories of the baby can make grieving hard, as there is a need first to establish some separate idea of the baby's identity (perhaps through photographs) to facilitate grief. Feelings may be intense, but are confused. Knowing this, the hospital social worker and colleagues attached to a maternity unit will attempt to help parents to have some control of the ways in which the tragedy is managed, and some reminders of their baby.

In cases of sudden or accidental death of an older child, a social worker may be involved at the time of death as part of a hospital team. We know that subsequent grieving is strongly affected by the ways in which the death and its initial aftermath are handled. In hospices, there is much attention paid to this in order to facilitate grieving (Herd 1990; Sheldon 1997; Monroe in Oliviere *et al.* 1998: 132f). In acute hospital settings, staff are more likely to be influenced by a need to 'get on'.

Where the death of a child has been expected, those workers from hospital or community teams who were involved before death may retain some involvement with bereaved parents, and the continuity of this relationship with someone who knew their child can be very important. Outside specialist palliative care services, however, social workers are not usually able to take on emotional support following the death of a service user. In adult services, this applies to home care managers and home carers as well as to social workers. Although they might attend the funeral and send a card to those bereaved, one visit after the death is likely to be the maximum that can be offered in a routine case, possibly accompanied by an invitation to contact the department if there should be a need in the future. The exception to this might be if the bereaved person had a reason to be a service user in his or her own right. In this case, ongoing contact would be maintained, and this could then possibly include some longer-term bereavement work.

The impact on those left after the death of a service user for whom there was a large amount of care may be enormous. Not only has the carer lost someone significant, whether a child with a disability or an aged parent or spouse, but they also lose a whole variety of professional 'visitors'. However welcome or unwelcome their intrusions have been, there is a substantial change after such a death, which has an impact in its own right. In the context of services for children with a severe disability, workers stress the great importance of providing respite and other support services earlier, when the day-to-day practical demands of physical care are great. This is partly in order to enable families to survive as a unit after such a death.

Social workers who were in practice in both community-based and hospital posts some 10–15 years ago tell a different story, which often included an ongoing bereavement service for those known to them through the death of a client. They speak of this now as 'a luxury' which would not now be possible for most mainstream services. Much could be learned in such situations from specialist colleagues. Although the culture of specialist palliative care recognises the legitimacy of grieving, bereavement follow-up is not necessarily offered to all, and often it is supervised volunteers who undertake this work. In mainstream and in specialist services, it may be necessary to use a single visit to assess vulnerability and risk. Bourne and Callus (in Oliviere *et al.* 1998: 122f) outline risk factors that distinguish the level of support offered. These include the presence of dependent family members, sudden death, family conflict, suicide risk. They also point to grief in which there is no 'ebb and flow' – a factor that is reminiscent of Stroebe and Schut's argument (1999) that pathology in grieving may relate to disturbance of oscillation (see section 6.3.1 above). Assessment is a key feature of the social work and social care role, whatever the setting.

In the examples that follow, service users were already in some form of contact with social care services. A care worker describes this situation in a small residential unit for four people with a learning disability.

■ Margaret had known Emily for a long time. They had moved together from a large hospital for people with learning disabilities into a small group home. Emily's death was very sudden. For a long time afterwards, Margaret was very withdrawn, both at the day centre and at home. She had sudden uncharacteristic bursts of anger, usually directed at staff.

In residential services for older people, bereavement affects three groups of people: relatives (who are not service users themselves) and fellow residents (who are), as well as staff. Fellow residents and staff may have known the service user for some years, as the profile of those in residential care indicates (section 5.1.3 above). Many homes have written policies and procedures setting out how a death and its immediate aftermath is to be handled. The ways in which fellow residents are informed may vary considerably. In my discussions with practitioners, most spoke of the importance of giving fellow residents the chance to say 'goodbye' in some way, either before the body was removed or through later discussion or ritual.

- When someone dies, we go round and tell others in the group. They have different reactions. Some say 'Don't forget to tell me when the funeral is' or 'I'd like to see the relatives when they come'. Some seek out a relative; others go into hiding. We try to follow that up informally later.

In relation to relatives, they reported that whilst some continue to visit the home, perhaps to see staff or other residents with whom their relative was friends, others do not wish to return. This is also true of hospices; whilst some relatives return for bereavement care and form strong relationships, others seem to wish to leave the experience behind. This is often a measure of their involvement with the unit prior to the death.

Work with bereaved relatives and with fellow residents after a death does not always conform to expectations. With regard to relatives, there might be conflict over disclosure or disposal, as these examples illustrate.

- One lady, apparently very religious, over 100-years-old, was a strong member of the local church, always went to communion. When she died, her relative insisted on a non-religious service.

- One relatively young woman's husband has lung cancer. We know he won't last long, but he refuses to have his wife told, so his wife is very angry and can see no reason for being here. Every now and then she calls a taxi to go home. He won't talk about it. This is an enormous problem for us because we cannot talk to her openly about his death. She is mentally rather than physically frail, and already has behavioural problems, but neither we nor the medical profession know how she will deal with his death.

The first example raised issues of loyalty and allegiance to the service user after her death, whilst the second is about staff members' concerns for the resident both in the present and in her future bereavement.

The other issue particular mentioned by some heads of home is the apparent lack of grief shown by many older residents at the death of a fellow resident. Without research that asks service users about the reasons for such apparent disinterest, it is not possible to say whether this reflects a culture in which relationships are not fostered, or a choice on the part of residents. In support of the latter suggestion, experienced staff members pointed out that people coming into residential care are an increasingly aged and frail population, many of whom have lived alone for years before reluctantly accepting this final move. Should it surprise us if they do not choose to form close relationships with others with whom they may have little in common? This observation should not, however, detract from recognition of such relationships that are formed, and the subsequent grief for a survivor when these relationships are broken through death.

8.1.3   Specialist Bereavement Services and Community Initiatives

There is no national policy or strategy relating to the provision of specialist bereavement services in Great Britain (Faulkner 1993; NABS 1999). Faulkner argues that 'the main problem in the bereavement services at present is the lack of agreement in the health service of what should be offered, by whom and for how long. This has resulted in a hotch-potch of services' (1993: 73). She points to risks both to bereaved people and to volunteers of a lack of co-ordinated support.

Ambiguity concerning whether bereavement and grief are – or are not – to be treated like illnesses for which either preventive or remedial intervention is routinely required, is responsible for some of the confusion. Faulkner herself assumes both that bereavement work is a professional activity in which 'professional skills are required to assess the bereaved person's ability to cope' (1993: 77) and that such services as are provided should be provided by the health service. Both assumptions are questionable. This reinforces her own point that service development is hampered by a lack of agreement about some basic issues.

Standards of training, supervision and practice are bound to vary between organisations, given the great variety of initiatives that exists. Even within one well-established service, the national CRUSE Bereavement Care charity, there is intense current debate as to appropriate

levels in relation to such matters. The level of ability and existing qualifications of volunteers varies considerably across the country, and some
local branches have resisted moves by the centre to 'professionalise' the
service. Yet public expectations have risen considerably from the days
when CRUSE started as a mutual support organisation for widows –
and with them, threats of litigation. Matters of terminology such as
whether visitors are named 'counsellors' or befrienders' reflect debates
in this as in other areas of voluntary service (Tyndall 1993).

In the face of such diversity, what can be said about services in the
UK that exist primarily to respond to the grief of people following
bereavement? Awareness of services and access to them are important
issues. Certain categories of bereaved people are likely to be *offered* a
service, whilst others may not know what services are available. Those
who have been in touch with palliative care services before the death
are likely to be offered help in bereavement. We have already seen that
this is a minority of those who die, and skewed towards those where the
death was cancer related. Such services vary considerably in size, but
are likely to be offered by volunteers, and usually organised and
supported by the social work department of a hospice (Franklin 1989;
Harrison 1996; Brewer 1996; Sheldon 1997; Oliviere *et al*. 1998). Social
workers may themselves take on direct counselling work in the most
complex cases. There has been some evaluation of the effectiveness of
bereavement counselling services. This has reported both satisfaction
on the part of service users (Danbury 1996) and some effectiveness as
measured by use of GP services following bereavement (Relf 1997,
cited in Sheldon 1997).

In addition to working with children who are known to the hospice
through a relationship to the person who has died, a number of
hospices offer a wider service to bereaved children in the locality (e.g.
Firth in Oliviere *et al*. 1998: 86–92; St Christopher's Hospice 1998).
Other specialist services for bereaved children also exist, some linked
to an established charity or voluntary organisation, others established
as independent charities or initiatives. Referral routes to such specialist
services for bereaved children vary. Parents, carers, teachers and
professionals can usually all refer children. Many of these projects are
run by social workers; some by other professionals.

In work with those affected with HIV/AIDS, as in palliative care
services more generally, bereavement support may be also be offered to
survivors after a death has occurred. Others who are likely to be offered
bereavement support are people whose grief leads to other problems,
be they behavioural or medical, as already noted in relation to services

for children. Such referral is likely to come through medical services – either the GP who might refer a patient to a counselling service within the practice, or psychiatric services if the disturbance has been sufficiently extreme to bring the person to the attention of such a service. One unusual initiative, worthy of special mention, is a bereavement group run in a closed women's prison (Woolfenden 1997).

If grief does not cause disturbance to others, it is likely to be left to the individual or their informal carers to identify a need for help and to find ways to access it. CRUSE bereavement care accepts only self-referrals – a way of ensuring that the person has himself or herself taken the first step in engaging with the helping process. It is not uncommon, however, for a professional or a relative or friend to have suggested that the person seeks such help. 'Bereavement forums' have been set up at a regional level in various areas to provide better information about local services and to facilitate access to them. Few of these services are proactive, however; the initiative has to be taken by the person who is bereaved, or someone close to them, both in relation to finding an appropriate source of help and in making contact. In running the smaller services, much depends on local interests, enthusiasm and the ability to secure funding. Social care workers (along with other professionals) play a part in many, either as direct providers or in a co-ordinating, training or advisory capacity.

The one area in which national policy guidelines do exist is in relation to disaster situations (Disasters Working Party 1991). These were set up after a review of the response of agencies to large-scale incidents that took place at the end of the 1980s. Then in 1996, sixteen children and their teacher were shot at Dunblane in Scotland. The co-ordinated response to this situation was based upon plans that had been initiated as a result of lessons learned through earlier situations and the guidelines that had been written by the Local Authorities concerned. These guidelines recognise a number of important principles that may have wider significance. Firstly, they advocate a proactive service for those who are most immediately affected. Secondly, they place responsibility for co-ordination of services not with health but with social care agencies, seeing this as an extension of their normal role in offering community support (Disasters Working Party 1991). The provision of a proactive service is unusual for social care, and accounts of such services (such as Tumelty 1990; Newburn 1993) discuss the difficulties that many social workers have had in adjusting to this. They also demonstrate, however – on the basis of user comments and feedback – that this was necessary in the context of grief that paralysed many involved.

The characteristics of individual grief reactions in disaster situations are not essentially different from that experienced in any bereavement, although there are differences that arise from issues such as scale, media involvement and the prolonged investigation procedures (Mead 1996). One argument for proactive care lies in the characteristic psychological experiences of early shock, numbness and denial in early bereavement. Others lie in the tendency of people to fail to recognise or to deny their own need of help, perhaps feeling that others are more badly affected (Newburn 1993). Such tendencies are common in all bereavement, and might lead us to suggest that services that rely upon those who are grieving to seek help for themselves are not the most likely to be effective.

To offer a proactive service in bereavement, service providers must have some link to the death event: this is the basis upon which service users in touch with palliative care services are offered a bereavement service, and is also the case in disaster situations. In everyday situations, three main community-based organisations play a key role in relation to death: the general practitioner, the undertaker and the church or other faith group. This section concludes, therefore, by describing two separate local initiatives. The first represents a growing trend – the development by churches or other faith bodies of a visiting service for those who are bereaved. This service is run by volunteers who receive support but no formal training. The second is, as far as I am aware, unique, but may represent a pattern for the future. This is a social work service offered for bereaved persons as part of a primary health care practice. It is delivered and organised by a paid and fully-trained social worker. Although not necessarily typical of services across the country, these two particular services are practical examples of community-based initiatives, as well as being examples of services that are offered on a routine, proactive basis.

The church-based visiting service is offered as an extension of the service of the priest who conducts funerals in a local parish church. A single visit is made by a 'bereavement visitor' to the bereaved person a little while after the funeral, with the offer of further visits if the person would like this. This is perhaps best viewed as an expression of community support, rather than as a counselling service. For some people who are bereaved, this may be very important.

The other service is offered by the social worker attached to a GP practice, as part of their preventive health services (Seymour 1997). An initial visit is made by the social worker, with others to follow should this be considered useful, either by the service user or the social worker. By visiting in this routine way, there is no suggestion that the person may be failing to cope. It is offered as 'after care' on a routine basis, but does, as a professional service, give an opportunity for a trained worker to pick up particular difficulties should these exist, together with establishing a relationship should the person feel a need for help later. Like home carers or care managers working for the local authority, members of the primary health care team do not usually themselves offer a 'follow up' service in cases of bereavement. Where they have been involved in support of someone dying at home, district nurses or GPs might make a single visit to a bereaved relative, but not more than this. Many primary health care teams do now employ counsellors, who might see patients presenting with problems that relate to bereavement, but this again is a service that relies upon the development and identification of difficulties by the person who is bereaved.

In the practice that employs a social worker specifically to offer bereavement follow-up there is also a counsellor, but the social worker sees her service as very different. The social work service is preventive, and there is preliminary evidence to suggest an association with reduced later health problems (Seymour 1997). It also offers practical as well as emotional support, including help with benefits and other matters, which the counselling service does not offer.

■ Thomas was a retiring man who had lived with his mother all his life. Although her death was not unexpected, it was quite sudden and had left a considerable vacuum in his life. It surprised him that he was finding it difficult to concentrate, as he had at times looked forward to the freedom of being on his own with only his own needs to attend to. His mother had become very demanding in her later years, and he had had to cut his working hours down so that he could look after her. From being a very careful tidy man, he realised that he had in the weeks since the funeral rather neglected the housework, but he didn't seem to have the energy to do much. He was at first suspicious of the woman who called from the doctor's surgery, but was reassured when she said that the call was a routine one made to all registered with the surgery as part of their follow-up service. The GP had been very good to his mother, even though he himself rarely went to the doctor.

The next section discusses the social care response in this and in the other situations described.

8.2   The Social Care Response

In the accounts that practitioners have given of their responses to the situations used as illustrations, three elements can be identified. These three elements will be used as an organising framework in this section. First is recognition of grief and of the need to grieve. Secondly, there is often some sense of accompaniment in this process. This has many facets; it may be practical or emotional accompaniment. It is about being held, about people who can stay with you through darkness and disorganisation. Often it is about hearing the story many times, or about being a 'witness'. Lastly, there is a need for acceptance and sometimes for practical help in moving on at different stages through bereavement – not just in a final sense. Not all services offer all three elements; sometimes intervention is very short-term, as we have seen, and the worker comes in at a particular part of the bereaved person's journey.

Although these elements seem at first sight to correspond to 'stages' or a 'beginning, middle and end' of the process of grieving, this is not so. They are put forward here as different possible aspects of the helper's role. Recognition by others of grief and the need to grieve may be as important many months after the event as it is in the time after the death, although there are particular issues around the time of death for professional carers, as we shall see. The third element has links with the 'restoration orientation' described by Stroebe and Schut (1999), which takes place throughout the grieving process and not as a final stage. It is also particularly relevant to the role of those in social care, whose work often involves helping people to work on practical aspects of 'getting their life together again', sometimes because other circumstances require this. Accompaniment and 'being a witness' are reminiscent of Walter's model of 'bereavement as biography', and it is interesting that professional workers often see this as an important aspect of their role, despite the fact that it is informal carers who play the largest part in this (Walter 1996).

By showing how these three aspects of responding to bereavement are manifest in practice settings, I hope to identify some differences between specialist and mainstream services, as well as some of the difficulties that may arise for mainstream practitioners wishing to be more sensitive in responding to grief. In some situations, the practitioner seeking to advocate for a service user will need to be assertive concerning these responses, which may sit uneasily with other pressures and agendas.

8.2.1   Recognising and Endorsing the Need to Grieve

This may be the greatest single contribution that a practitioner can make. It is perhaps most powerfully illustrated in two of the examples in which social workers were faced with sudden death. In these two contrasting settings, there was much busyness and activity and a great danger that a unique opportunity would be missed. The responses of the workers concerned are outlined below.

■ The coroner's officers had already finished their examination and the body of the daughter was ready to be taken for post-mortem examination before the social worker realised the implications for the elderly mother who was still not speaking. Somewhat hesitantly, the worker asked the police and coroner's officials if they would stop and take the daughter's body into another room in order for her mother to say her farewells. Objections were raised; all the officials concerned were busy, with other cases to attend; this would cause delay and inconvenience. Moreover, the efforts of the police had been directed at keeping the mother from distress, and this seemed calculated to upset her. The worker insisted, embarrassed, but confident of the importance of this, and the mother was led into the front room, where she could touch her daughter's body. Immediately, she burst into tears and started to talk about her daughter. The social worker later arranged alternative accommodation for her. Each time they met, this woman said how grateful she was to have had this opportunity to bid her daughter farewell.

The setting for the second example was in a hospital Accident and Emergency Department.

■ Amid the activity carrying on around the mother and her dead child, with police waiting to start an investigations as soon as efforts to save the baby were clearly in vain, the social worker said to the senior nurses 'We must respect this moment.' Then the nurses, chaplain and social worker gathered around the baby's bed for a short service. They took a photo of the baby, and a lock of his hair for the mother to keep. For a few moments the activity and questioning all ceased, whilst the mother had an opportunity to begin grieving for her child.

In the second instance, it had just taken one person to recognise this need to grieve, and others readily complied. It might just as easily have been the chaplain or a nurse. In the first, there was some conflict. Sometimes it will be other social work colleagues who are pushing to 'move on'. It is not easy to insist, often against formidable opposition, on the need to 'stop the action' and create a space for grief to begin. There *are* often other pressing things that need to be done. In the second example, there was a later investigation into the baby's death, in which the action of the social worker was commended.

It is important too to recognise that this is a proactive role on behalf of the bereaved person, as it is often a time when that person is unable to speak or to be assertive on their own behalf. It is not, then, about empowering the client at this point, but about acting *for* them on the basis of knowledge of the general needs of people in this situation. Another example underlines this point. In this instance, the worker involved was a community nurse by training, working in a res- idential school for children with profound disabilities. She had agreed to share with the parents of a dying child the task of holding him as he died in hospital – a vigil of several days. As it happened, she was the one with the boy when he died, and his father was not in the hospital. Nurses tried to take the child's body from her, seeking to 'get on'. She insisted on continuing to hold him until his father came. Asked 'how long will it be?', she replied 'as long as it takes'. The father arrived to find his dead son held, as he had wished, by a trusted person who had cared enough to insist on resisting pressure to 'tidy up'. In palliative care, management of the time immediately after death is carefully handled because staff appreciate just how significant this will be in relation to subsequent bereavement (Sheldon 1997; Oliviere *et al.* 1998). This is one area where mainstream social care differs from specialist palliative care. In the former, practitioners may have to fight to get agreement to practices that respect this need to grieve. In specialist palliative care, on the other hand, systems are geared towards doing this.

Yet this recognition of the need to grieve is not limited to the way in which the death itself is handled. Such recognition may be necessary much later. We know from accounts of response in disaster situations that three of six identified barriers to receiving help are related to a person's lack of recognition of their own need to grieve (Newburn 1996). Thus, people affected may feel numb and not recognise their own distress; they may have a self-image that sees coping as important, or they may see their own needs and distress as trivial compared with that of others. Although this comparative element may seem more obvious in a situation that has affected many people, it is also common for other people who are bereaved to 'put down' their own needs, saying, for example, 'there's many worse off than me'. In disaster situations, a generally proactive approach has been adopted, as already identified, and the same is true of the two community services discussed in the previous section. Yet even in a service such as CRUSE that is not itself proactive, people who refer themselves may start by being very diffident about their need either to grieve or to receive help to do so. It is the counsellor's job then to insist that grieving is important, and that there are times when we all need help to create opportunities for this.

Many of the examples of services for children required recognition by others of the need of the child to grieve, and often some thought about how this might be facilitated. In relation to the situation where a member of staff had died, the remaining staff of West Lodge, and the social workers for the children living there, had a responsibility to consider how the children might be facilitated in their distress. Would the children be taken to the funeral? Who would accompany them? Given that residential care staff would themselves be grieving, there was a good case to be made for this being undertaken by field social workers. This is a different kind of 'stopping the action'; perhaps less dramatic, but still requiring that grief and the need to grieve are recognised and taken seriously in children for whom the Department has a statutory responsibility.

In the cases of Nathan and Stephen, referred to earlier (section 8.1.1), any assessment of their future accommodation needs has to take account of their current distress and consider how this might be handled. For Richard and Brian (also section 8.1.1), their grief could not easily be ignored. In both instances it seemed to be behind their aggressive behaviour. In Richard's case, his temper tantrums were managed by his foster carers, who encouraged him to talk about his baby brother, of whom he had a photo. They also encouraged him to talk about his brother with his mother when he saw her. His behaviour steadily improved. The link between this and his grief in relation to his brother's death was demonstrated when Richard gave a baby-hat, which had belonged to his brother, to his foster mother for safekeeping. Brian's situation was very different. His father had died the previous year. He was not able to discuss his father with his mother as her memories were of an abusive partner, and it was difficult to share these with her son. Professional bereavement counselling was arranged to enable Brian to work through his very intense feelings about his father.

One social worker in a hospital setting working with people who have harmed themselves stresses the link between early loss or grief and subsequent self-harm. She emphasises that children often need adults who can help them to grieve. This is endorsed by responses from a range of specialists in bereavement work with children (*Lifeline* 1999: 11–19). Social workers with responsibility for children's services need to take this on board and work actively at facilitating grief, not only through calling in specialist counsellors (although this may be needed), but in their own day-to-day practice also. The statement of what bereaved children need (above, section 6.5) is applicable in many settings.

It is not only children who need such help. Margaret, mourning her friend Emily (section 8.1.2 above), needed staff at the day centre and in the group home who recognised her need to grieve. One trainer reports on a day working with staff and service users in a day centre for people with learning disabilities. The focus of the training was on 'saying goodbye'. Staff reported a marked reduction in disruptive behaviour amongst the service users following this day's training.

Sometimes the need for grief to be recognised is very low-key. Thomas (section 8.1.3 above) felt much better after the visit of the social worker from the GP practice. He had spent time talking about his mother and how much he missed her, and about some of her funny ways. Before the worker had called, he had been wondering what was wrong with him, although he would never have gone to the surgery or anywhere else for help. Now he realised that many people feel the same way after a death. Much bereavement visiting or counselling of a voluntary nature has such endorsement and recognition of the validity of grieving as its main purpose.

In specialist settings, whether in the statutory or voluntary sector, the specialist service itself by its existence states that grief is important. In mainstream services, this may not be so. The main 'business' of the organisation does not relate to grieving and sometimes it may seem that it does not even allow for it. Siddell, Katz and Komorary's study of residential care (1998) demonstrates, for example, how an emphasis in social care for older people upon residential care as a place to *live* has, to a certain extent, worked against attention being given in these settings to dying. In other services, such as children's services, dying and bereavement are not a main focus, despite the fact that they occur. Community care legislation has led to a focus upon needs for care in a practical sense, with an emphasis upon questions of resources. The mainstream worker therefore has often to deliberately create recognition of the importance of grieving, which can seem to distract attention from the main business of service purchasers and providers alike.

It is important to remember that this recognition does not have to take a long time. It is not about counselling, and is not incompatible with the purchaser role. It also needs to be acknowledged by managers as an important issue. In the situation at West Lodge (section 8.1.1 above), for example, managers needed to be asking how the children's need to grieve would be handled in relation to the funeral, and who would accompany them if they wished to go.

8.2.2 Accompaniment in Grief: The Role of Witness

In speaking of bereavement work, a number of practitioners spoke of 'staying with chaos', of 'holding' the grieving individual or family. Ann Couldrick (1995) uses the phrase 'cradling' to describe 'the professional's cradling of the bereaved family' after the death of a parent, and this term was used by one of the workers I spoke to, too. In disaster work, workers describe the need to hear the story, over and over (Mead 1996), and to be with the bereaved and with survivors both in a general sense and, critically, as they attend inquests and other legal proceedings. This is like two of the factors mentioned in Chapter 4 concerning the worker's response to dying. There I spoke of 'being there; the gift of presence and of dependability' and of offering time and attention, both factors that are crucial for work with bereaved people too. In disaster follow-up, Newburn identifies 'personal support' as a critical aspect of the social work service offered after Hillsborough, together with practical support. This includes accompaniment and befriending: 'essentially "being there" for people, not just in the early days, but later on when other sources of support have disappeared or when particularly stressful occasions arise' (Newburn 1993: 122).

'Being there' is almost a defining feature of residential care, whether for children or adults. To be effective for the person who is grieving, this needs to go beyond a physical presence to acknowledgement of emotional needs. Care workers can offer such acknowledgement in many ways. Too often, ongoing emotional care is lost in the business of 'getting on'. The old lady who sits alone lost in thought or crying can easily be ignored by care assistants who are rushed off their feet. June Wright (section 8.1.2 above) had been unable to attend her son's funeral, which had been held abroad. She needed to talk about her son, and welcomed the suggestion of putting together a scrapbook of his letters and pictures of where he had lived. The social worker encouraged her to tell the story and to share her memories of him, as well as helping to increase her current range of contacts. She became her companion in the process of creating the story of his life.

Being a 'witness' is something that has also emerged from my discussions with practitioners. This has two senses. Firstly, in relation to work that has covered the time before as well as after a death, a number of workers spoke of the way in which families used to refer to them to endorse a memory or to share it. This was particularly so in relation to services for children with a disability, where a worker may have seen a first achievement or smile. In one instance, a worker remembered a child who had a progressively disabling condition, where the parents would recall her prior abilities. In others, it was just a case of remembering the child. In some instances, the family may look for validation that they have 'done all they could', before the death. The worker who had been there before could not only share memories of their child but could endorse their own efforts and performance.

This is so in bereavement counselling also. One thing that the counsellor can offer is reassurance concerning 'progress' for the bereaved person, who may feel lost in their own overwhelming feelings and needs someone outside the situation to say 'you have come a long way, you are coping'. This is not about some sort of accurate measurement against a scale of prescribed reactions, but reassurance that all is well (Walter 1999). Many bereaved people find it reassuring in this sense to read accounts by others of their own bereavement (Holloway 1990).

This sense of being a witness came over very strongly from the account of a social work student who visited Lily (section 8.1.2 above) shortly after her husband's funeral. His role was to conduct an assessment of her needs. He became drawn into the telling of her story of her husband's life and death. In terms of Walter's description of bereavement as biography (1996), he felt that he had become cast as a member of the 'audience'. Walter suggests that professionals cannot enter into the process of biography creation that occurs after a death, but he ignores the fact that many did in fact know the deceased before death, and also perhaps overlooks the role of the 'reader' or 'audience' in his literary analogy. Bereavement counselling is often like being the audience at a rehearsal; an opportunity for the bereaved person to 'try out' the story of their changing feelings.

This role of 'being alongside' also involves recognising and accepting the continuing effects upon the bereaved person of their grief. Sometimes it does not seem to offer any prospect of moving on. This was the case for both Florence and Samuel (section 8.1.2 above). In terms of Stroebe and Schut's 'dual process model', Florence did not wish to focus upon restoration. The prior deaths of her children meant that there was for, for her, no future. In this instance the social work task was to make practical arrangements for her care. As for Samuel, accompaniment seems to involve little more that practical and physical care. It would be wrong to give the impression that attention to grief always leads to a happier outcome. As many social care workers know too well, some people do feel that their losses are so great that there is little to live for. For them there is sometimes merely a grim satisfaction in having people around who will listen to their sadness, anger or distress, and help them to be as comfortable as possible. This too is accompaniment.

Whilst the bereavement counsellor, particularly in a voluntary capacity, and those in residential or home care may be able to take on an accompanying role, this may be harder for the field social worker. Again there is another agenda. The worker conducting an assessment may understand the effects of grief upon a person's ability to care for himself, or herself, but they still have to help that person to make decisions about the future. We have already seen that children and those who are physically dependent upon others may have to make changes at a time of intense grief. There may also be conflicts between the needs of bereaved members of the same family. Whilst part of the role of the worker is to validate the feelings of the bereaved person, their actions (or lack of action) may cause difficulties for others or for themselves in the longer term. Thus, whilst one would wish to stay with a person through chaos, letting this proceed at the pace of the person who is bereaved, there is sometimes a conflicting need to help a person to recognise the claims of others. This was so for Marjorie, whose need to grieve for her mother led to a wish to visit her grave daily, preventing the whole family from ever having a holiday. In this instance, the task of the worker involved was to help her to see how her own grief was affecting those around her, and then to find other ways of maintaining a connection with her mother.

8.2.3 Support in Relation to Questions of 'Re-engagement'

As we have seen from Chapter 6, 'moving on' is a vexed question in relation to theoretical understandings of grieving. In the accounts of those who are bereaved, it is an area of potential conflict with others. On the one hand, individuals may encounter resistance from others if they 'move on' too soon: Newburn reports an incident where there was explicit community 'disapproval' of one woman who found a new boy-friend after her partner had been killed in the Hillsborough disaster (Newburn 1993: 82). More commonly, bereaved people speak of the expectation of those around them that they will 'move on' much sooner than they are ready to do. This is an example of the regulation or 'policing' of grief by informal carers, described by Walter (1999).

Stroebe and Schut's model (1999) offers a way of understanding the social care role, since this often concerns restoration activities; not always because the bereaved person themselves wishes to 'move on'. As we have seen, a referral often arises due to a practical problem, such as a need for alternative accommodation following a death. Rarely can the worker say 'wait until you feel ready' in such circumstances. Social care workers must find ways of working on restoration whilst also acknowledging the reality and depth of loss. Faced with the necessity for decisions and change, there is a need for good support. Most work with children and young people following loss and separation involves this tension. Supporting tentative new beginnings is as much a part of the role of a helper as allowing time to cry or to focus upon loss.

This chapter began by asking why there was any need for professional involvement with those who are bereaved. My answer to this was, firstly, that there are times when professional helpers are amongst those people who are already involved with a person who is bereaved. This is particularly so in situations offering residential or day care. Where this is the case, it is important for formal as much as for informal carers to respond if possible in a helpful rather than a destructive way. Indeed, to do so can be seen as part of an overall duty of care on the part of service providers. A second reason that can be put forward for specific intervention by social care workers in relation to bereavement is that there may be particular reasons why informal care does not or cannot offer adequate support or help. Some of these reasons relate to overall cultural or social factors, others are linked to particular circum-stances. For example, a death situation can itself overwhelm or destroy informal systems of care, at least temporarily, when those who would offer support are themselves grieving. In old age, many people find they have severely reduced social networks, or that these were maintained by or revolved around the very person who has died.

Social care workers need therefore to be able to respond to grief in situations where there is no adequate informal response, or where this response is, for any reason, insufficient for the bereaved person's needs. In some instances, no amount of effort can make the informal care system adequate, because its very closeness and familiarity is what gives rise to difficulties. The status of the professional as 'outsider' is often very important (Newburn 1993: 118), and may help the primary care network to function more effectively. As family and systems workers demonstrate, informal caring systems may themselves be dysfunctional for individuals (Sutcliffe, Tufnell and Cornish 1998).

8.3   Issues of Training and Support

Like parenting, the important work of being with other people at times of bereavement is something for which no special training is necessarily seen to be needed – it is an aspect of our shared humanity and care for each other. Informal carers receive information and knowledge from lay sources, such as books, magazines and television programmes, some of which have an explicitly educative function. There are then those organisations and initiatives that explicitly seek to offer some kind of help. In mutual help groups (Walter 1999), the qualification for would-be helpers is personal experience. In other services, such as CRUSE Bereavement Care, the counsellor's experience of bereavement is not an issue – qualification for the work is based upon training. As already discussed, matters of training and of the levels of supervision required for such work may be the features that distinguish one type of intervention from another. At one end of the spectrum of voluntary provision, we see a move towards national standards and accreditation (NABS, CRUSE) within those bodies which receive voluntary or public funding. At the other end, there are some local initiatives that have no formal requirements for training. It is important that professionals and paid workers recognise and respect the lay knowledge that forms the basis for informal care and for some voluntary initiatives. It is equally important, however, that they ask about the level of formal training and support that volunteers receive. Such information will enable them to work effectively with volunteers, and to avoid inappropriate referrals.

What do social care practitioners say about the skills, knowledge, training and support that underpin their work? Are different or additional skills needed by those who specialise in work with bereaved people? Are social care workers in the mainstream of care equipped already for the role of responding to the needs of bereaved clients, or is extra training needed? The comments made to me in relation to these issues fall into three main categories: knowledge and skills; issues concerned with the use of self – the personal/professional boundary;

and comments about aspects of the role or about policy and practice in the workplace.

In relation to knowledge and skills, most of the professionally qualified social workers that I have asked have said that all the basic elements of their qualifying training were as applicable in work with bereaved people as in any other area of social care (see also Sheldon 1998). Knowledge of psychological processes, an understanding of social policy and social structure and skills relating to assessment and intervention were all stressed. Some practitioners felt that there had been too little in their training about death and grief, and that this is a central issue in all areas of social care that should receive more attention. Counselling and communication skills were seen as very important, and some commented on a need to resist any move away from seeing these as central in all social care work. There was concern that some moves in social work education and training have been towards competencies and practical skills and away from an emphasis upon regard for the emotions and a holistic approach. This is an ongoing debate within social work education (Eraut 1994; Fish 1999).

There was little doubt amongst those practitioners I interviewed that emotional components in training are essential at all levels. This can be as much about process (how topics are taught) as about curriculum content. There is scope, too, for use of the creative arts within direct work – use of art, music and movement. These skills have tended to be overlooked within social care. Bright (1996) writes about grief from the perspective of a music therapist, and others look at the use of movement and dance (Warren 1993). Sheldon (1998) also mentions the use of creative approaches, as well as the need for training that is multi-disciplinary.

Most workers had supplemented their own basic training by specialist courses concerning bereavement. Some workers had extra qualifications as fully trained counsellors or psychotherapists, but it was noticeable that such specialists did not see this as the most important element in their training or skills base, rather as something that enabled them to take on more complex work. The ability to reflect upon practice and to use the self was defined by many as centrally important for anyone undertaking this work, whether or not they had formal professional qualifications.

In particular areas of work, additional appropriate training or knowledge was seen as necessary. For work in the field of HIV and AIDS, for example, there is an enormous amount of medical knowledge that has to be constantly updated. Workers in residential care said they would value the development of skills concerning management of difficult behaviours; this in work with young and old service users. Concern was expressed that many front-line workers in social care lack formal training even in basic issues; this puts them and their clients at risk. Whilst professional social work training did not always offer enough depth, it was essential underpinning; the more recent NVQ qualifications were seen as offering a way for other social care workers to gain some of these skills and knowledge at a different level.

Whatever the level of training, support is crucial for care workers in emotionally difficult situations. A Probation Officer tells the following story.

■ For over a year, I was working with a young man of 21 who was on a three-year Probation Order following a conviction for arson. He had mild learning difficulties and had been involved in chronic substance misuse, mainly solvents. Over the year his interests settled and his self-destructive behaviour began to change. Then he died through choking on his own vomit. So much professional and personal investment seemed to be lost, just at the point where there was hope of progress.

The worker comments that in probation and youth justice work, many service users live dangerous lives, and some will die. Where do you pitch your personal relationship with them, and how do you manage your own grief after a death?

This leads us to the second category identified in practitioners' accounts: the use of self, and comments upon managing the personal/professional boundary. Here a tension is evident, and it is clear that the 'message' is about recognising and managing this tension, and not about resolving difficulties by emphasising one side at the expense of the other. On the one hand, workers said that you must 'be yourself', 'be real', and 'be human'. A level of personal involvement was seen by many as essential if you were to be an effective practitioner working with grieving people. Moreover, your own personal experience of life and loss were seen as an essential backdrop for the work. Several workers told of how their own experiences had been of value in helping them to relate to service users, and many spoke of the need to cry with people and to 'go beyond' the professional role, using the resources of their own experience, personality and emotions. This was not limited to social care workers: a chaplain spoke powerfully of the need for all sorts of workers – nurses, police, ambulance crews – to rediscover and allow their own feelings to be part of their work, if they were to really help people in the midst of grief.

Yet the dangers for the worker of personal involvement were also stressed. For example, home carers were reported to find it hard when a mother with young children died; a measure of their own emotional investment and identification. Part of what is of help to the service user is feeling that the worker can 'cope'; this is as true in residential care of older people, as in disaster situations (Newburn 1993). If the worker is too involved or affected by grief, they cease to be an outsider, and the grieving person may start to feel a responsibility for their feelings and reactions too. Part of being a professional is having another place to take one's own reactions – something which underlines the importance of supervision and support.

This tension is not a new one for social work. In 1961, Biestek drew up seven principles of casework, amongst which we find 'controlled emotional involvement'. This succinctly highlights both the need to be involved emotionally and the need to be in control of and able to manage this. Practitioners stressed above all the ability to recognise and accept one's own feelings and reactions as legitimate, to be self-aware and able to reflect upon work experience and to be able to use the self creatively within the helping relationship. Current social work training emphasises all these qualities, although it is sometimes questionable whether programmes do enough to foster them.

Support and supervision are essential ingredients if this ideal is to be realised. This brings us to the third strand in practitioners' comments, which concerned their role, and organisational and policy matters. Again we hit a tension or paradox. There is a need for practitioners to accept not only their own helplessness in many situations – 'we cannot always make it better' – but also the ambiguities of the social work role. In respect of the latter, such ambiguities were seen to be part of the history but also part of the strength of social care, which has always been 'riding two horses' as servant of the state and advocate of the people (Lorenz 1994). This is an uncomfortable place, but one where social care needs to be. The distinctiveness of the social work role lies in its breadth and lack of boundaries; this leads to overlap, but also to creativity and flexibility. Helplessness and lack of definition are not easy to accept. At the same time, there is a need for workers who are confident about their role, their reason for being there and about what they can offer. This observation was made by specialist palliative care workers, a social work trainer and also an experienced team manager in a children and families team. It also comes strongly out of the work in response to disasters (Newburn 1993; Mead 1996), and is a feature of most pioneering care, such as voluntary initiatives for bereaved children (Stokes and Crossley 1995).

There was recognition by some of the need to accept other limits to their work, such as resource constraints. These should be honestly acknowledged and faced. Others, however, spoke of a need to resist some trends in social care which were seen to be undermining the service offered. There was a need, said many, to resist economic factors becoming the prime determinants of service; professional issues need to be heard. Thus some spoke with regret of what they saw as a recent abandonment of some of professional principles that need to guide policy; certain matters such as training and adequate staff support are essential, and not corners to be cut for financial savings. The service is either worth providing properly or should not be offered at all.

Let me offer examples of this that relate directly to the issues of grieving that have been discussed here. There has been a move to privatisation of home care services. This can be driven solely by financial considerations. It is essential that questions are also asked about levels of staff training and support if workers are to work with dying and bereaved people on a routine basis. In relation to care management and assessments of need, to what extent are workers expected to complete such work quickly in order to clear beds? Assessing a person who is grieving can take some time; listening to their concerns is part of the work, not a luxury. Are managers willing to support workers who want to do a thorough job that may involve 'stopping the action' at times? How quickly are beds in residential care filled after a death? Is the professional argument for giving residents and workers a little time to grieve even a part of the debate? Under arrangements to promote national standards in social care in England and Wales (see Care Standards Bill 1999), can we look to employing bodies (whether private, voluntary or statutory agencies) to protect and promote the well-being of service users who are grieving, or is cost-cutting the only agenda?

None of the workers I have interviewed wished to deny the realities of financial constraints. They did sometimes wonder, however, how far professional standards were being seen as of equal importance. Responding to grief is clearly not a wishy-washy emotional business at the level either of practice or of policy. It can involve the difficult task of resisting moves based solely on criteria such as 'moving on' or 'getting the job done'. To some extent, social work has always been about managing tensions and advocacy, and this is as true in work with people who are bereaved as in other areas of social care. Managers, as well as practitioners, need to be clear about the principles that underpin the work of the service, and some of this is about knowledge in relation to the needs of those who are grieving, as well as understanding of the need of staff for support.

Adequate support and supervision for staff is essential for staff responding to other people's grief. This is a non-negotiable aspect of service provision. For some respondents, it needed to be available from a source outside the workplace, but it is also about the way induction is handled for new staff, about work structures that are clear and supportive, and about ongoing opportunities to discuss and reflect upon work with colleagues. In most instances, such support was available to some extent, and many gave examples of good practice in this regard, whilst also speaking of fears that this might be eroded. One manager spoke of the importance of the way that personal staff bereavements are acknowledged and managed within the staff team. Staff members, like informal carers, need to feel that they have done what they could for a service user. Regular and effective supervision that gives time for emotional issues is critical. Literature concerning burn-out and absenteeism (e.g. Davidson and Foster 1995) reinforces a view that it is also cost-effective in the long run.

9

Responding to Grief: Conclusions for Social Care

Although those working in social care in the UK are familiar with constant reorganisation and change, the changes on the horizon at the start of the new millennium are likely to be more far reaching than ever before. Demographic and political changes have led to increasing need and rising expectations, unmatched by increases in resources. Social care workers make up approximately 5 per cent of the UK workforce, spanning all age groups and with a wide range of experience and training. These include a small number of highly specialised social workers in palliative care; and a larger number of professionally qualified social workers working in mainstream rather than specialist settings. Amongst social work students, there is interest in working with dying and bereaved people, but often little knowledge of the ways in which this is possible, outside specialist agencies.

I hope that the examples given in the course of this book will have given newcomers to the field some idea of the breadth and range of work to be done, and of its challenges. For those already in mainstream social care, I hope these examples will have stimulated a resolve to recognise and work with the grief that exists in the setting in which they work. If practitioners feel unsure whether bereavement or dying *are* issues for the service users they work with, perhaps it would be a good idea to find out, and to establish what policies and procedures in the workplace might apply to the care of dying or bereaved people. Sometimes just asking the question leads into thinking about how services might be improved.

Demonstrating and illustrating the ways in which social care workers are involved with dying and bereaved people was the first of my aims (section 1.2). In this chapter, I pull together some of the strands from preceding chapters by means of four questions about the relationship between social care and dying and bereavement. Firstly, why be involved with people who are dying or bereaved? Secondly, what can social care

workers contribute? Thirdly, what is necessary for us to do this effectively, and lastly, how is this particular to social care?

9.1 Why Should Social Care Workers be Involved with Those Who are Dying or Bereaved?

Two answers to this are apparent from preceding chapters. The first is
that we already *are* involved. This is not an area of work that is optional,
or extra in some way. Our work brings us into contact with many service
users who have experienced bereavement, and some who may be dying.
Knowing about dying and bereavement is, quite simply, part of the job.
Whether we are involved with someone for only a short time or over
many years, there will be times when we need to know how to respond
to grief in the context of the other work we are doing. Some of the most
critical and important interventions take only a moment; we do not
need time or vast resources to acknowledge someone's grief.

Secondly, there are times when there is a need for input from someone outside the informal care network. The government has suggested,
in the context of work on communal disasters, that social care is well
placed to offer such help. We should be accepting this as a vote of confidence and be creative about the ways in which we can offer a service in
less traumatic times, perhaps by supporting voluntary initiatives in our
area, and referring people to them. This may involve work as a member
of a liaison group or steering group for a local service. Identification of
unmet need and looking for ways to promote service developments are
all aspects of our role.

9.2 What Can Social Care Workers Do?

Both dying and bereavement can be thought of as transitional states or
processes. In the case of dying, this is a time of preparing to be perman-
ently separated from society and culture. In bereavement, the one who
grieves needs, after a while, to 're-engage' with life and other people.
Separation and loneliness are characteristic of both states. Yet for this
very reason, people have a great need to be supported in these lonely
and frightening times when they can often give little back.

In the case of dying, thinking in terms of managing the present, abandoning the future and maintaining a sense of connectedness for as long
as possible may help us to think about what can be offered. Managing

the present is often something with which social care workers are asked to help. Maintaining connectedness reminds us that there is no need for social death to occur or be reinforced early on. We need to offer as many opportunities as possible for people to participate in social life, even when they are dying.

In bereavement, there is a need to recognise and create space for grieving; to hear the story and to assist with restoration or re-engagement as appropriate. Often we can act as facilitators or brokers for people. We need to know about the self-help groups available, and help people to make contact should they wish to do so. This is not about imposing any timescale for re-engagement, but supporting what seems right to the person concerned. There can be conflicting needs within the informal network. We may be able to clarify what is happening and facilitate communication.

9.3   What Do We Need if We are to Do this Well?

We need to be convinced that grief matters, and clear about our own role, confident that we have something worthwhile to offer, even if the person concerned is unsure whether they want it. We need theoretical understanding of the grief process, matters to do with dying and good knowledge of local resources. We need the ability to listen, to advocate for the service user and to make links for them with other services as appropriate. Above all, we need to be open enough to share something of the service user's sorrow, whilst remaining strong enough to be dependable and a source of strength. To do this, adequate supervision and support are essential.

9.4   How is this Particular to Social Care?

In many ways it is not. The fact is, however, that social care workers tend to work with those who have little power and few social or economic resources. They are therefore both most subject to grief (Weiss 1991) and most powerless in face of it. The grief of those who have little social status or power (the very old, the young, those with a learning disability, those in prison), is often not heard or even acknowledged. Sadly, there is sometimes no one else to be a witness, to hear the story. In addition, those seeking to re-enter social life but who lack financial resources and/or knowledge of how the system works may need extra help to re-establish their lives after a death. Discrimination makes attempts at restoration hard and this needs to be challenged.

It has been my aim in this book to demonstrate that work with people who are dying or bereaved – although not particular to social care – fits extremely well with the remit of social care workers in mainstream settings. It is entirely compatible with the ways in which social care is defined. Recent theoretical understandings of the grief process place increased emphasis upon social processes, and there is much scope for intervention that is more broadly based than 'counselling'. In all this, social carers can have a vital role. Of course, this will often be through working in collaboration with colleagues from other disciplines, particularly with health workers.

For anyone who sees work with dying and bereaved people as a quiet 'backwater of social care' where there is an opportunity to practise social work 'as it used to be', think again. It is as challenging and demanding as any other area of practice. For both specialist and mainstream workers, forging real and essential links with colleagues in health will demand all the skills that a worker possesses. Overall, we have a brief for community care. Dying and bereavement are both community issues. There is no need to join a specialist team to work with dying or bereaved people; these are issues for us all.

Organisations

Contact a Family

170 Tottenham Court Road
London W1P 0HA

Tel: 020 7383 3555
e-mail: info@cafamily.org.uk

Exists to help families who care for children with any disability or special need, through advice, information and linking.

CRUSE Bereavement Care

126 Sheen Road
Richmond
Surrey TW9 1UR

Tel: 020 8940 4818

A national charity with groups in many parts of the UK offering bereavement counselling and social activities for bereaved people. *CRUSE Chronicle* is a monthly newsletter for bereaved people published by the organisation.

National Association of Bereavement Services (NABS)

20 Norton Folgate
London
E1 6DB

Tel: 020 7247 0617

Has since 1988 existed to act as a co-ordinating body for bereavement services nationally, operating a helpline for members of the public, and maintaining a database of information about services throughout the country. Its newsletter is *Lifeline*, which gives details of projects and services for bereaved people. See, for example, Summer 1999 edition, pp. 21–35, for details of a variety of children's services.

Bibliography

Ainsworth, M. D., Blehar, M. C., Waters, E. and Wall, S. (1978) *Patterns of Attachment* (New Jersey: Erlbaum).

Alcock, P. (1998) 'Labour in Power: 3. Social Exclusion', *Community Care*, 26 November–2 December, pp. 17–24.

Aldrich, C. (1974) 'Some Dynamics of Anticipatory Grief', in B. Schoenberg, A. Carr, A. Kutscher, D. Peretz and K. Goldberg (eds), *Anticipatory Grief* (London: Colombia University Press).

Anonymous (1997) 'The Stigma of Bereavement', *Lifeline*, no. 23 (Spring), pp. 22–3.

Antonovsky, A. (1987) *Unravelling the Mystery of Health* (London: Jossey-Bass Publishers).

Aries, P. (1974) *Western Attitudes Towards Death* (London: Marion Boyars).

Aries, P. (1981) *The Hour of Our Death* (London: Allen Lane).

Atkinson, D. and Williams, F. (eds) (1990) *Know Me As I Am* (London: Hodder & Stoughton).

Awoonor-Renner, S. (1993) 'I Desperately Needed to See My Son', in D. Dickenson and M. Johnson (eds), *Death, Dying and Bereavement* (London: Sage).

Barclay Committee (1982) *Social Workers: Their Roles and Tasks* (London: Bedford Square Press/National Institute for Social Work).

Barnard, P. and Kane, M. (1995) 'Voices from the Crowd – Stories from the Hillsborough Football Stadium Disaster', in S. Smith and M. Pennells (eds), *Interventions with Bereaved Children* (London: Jessica Kingsley Publishers).

Barnard, P. and Kane, M. (1996) 'Listening to the Voice of the Child: From Hillsborough to Liverpool Children's Project', in C. Mead (ed.), *Journeys of Discovery: Creative Learning from Disaster* (London: NISW).

Barry, N. (1989) 'When a Child Dies', *Social Work Today*, 8 June, p. 23.

Baulkwill, J. (1998) 'Single Session Group Work with Bereaved Children', in D. Oliviere, R. Hargreaves and B. Monroe (eds), *Good Practices in Palliative Care* (Aldershot: Ashgate), pp. 80–6.

Baum, J., Dominica, Sr F. and Woodward, R. (eds) (1990) *Listen, My Child Has a Lot of Living to Do* (Oxford: Oxford University Press).

Beloff, J. (1993) *Parapsychology, a Concise History* (London: The Athlone Press) chapter 2, Spiritualism.

Biestek, F. P. (1961) *The Casework Relationship* (London: Allen & Unwin).

Bishop, V. (ed.) (1997) *Clinical Supervision in Practice: Some Questions, Answers and Guidelines* (London: Macmillan).

Black, D. (1998) 'Bereavement in Childhood', *British Medical Journal*, vol. 316, 21 March, pp. 931–3.

Blackburn, A. M. (1989) 'Problems of Terminal Care in Elderly Patients', *Palliative Medicine*, vol. 3, pp. 203–6.

Bowlby, J. (1969) *Attachment and Loss, Volume I: Attachment* (London: Hogarth Press).

Bowlby, J. (1971) *Loss* (Harmondsworth: Penguin).

Bowlby, J. (1973) *Attachment and Loss, Volume II: Separation: Anxiety and Anger* (London: Hogarth Press).

Bowlby, J. (1980) *Attachment and Loss, Volume III: Loss, Sadness and Depression* (London: Hogarth Press).

Brent Bereavement Project (1998) Annual report, 1997–8, Willesden Community Hospital, Harlesden Road, London, NW10 3RY.

Brewer, G. (1996) 'Take Two', *Community Care*, 8–14 February.

Bright, R. (1996) *Grief and Powerlessness: Helping People Regain Control of Their Lives* (London: Jessica Kingsley Publishers).

Brodkey, H. (1996) Last published piece of writing, *Independent on Sunday*, 11 February.

Brodribb, C. and Smith, S. (1995) 'Quality Control', Inside Special Supplement on Terminal Illness, *Community Care*, 26 January–1 February, pp. 2–3.

Brown, G. and Harris, T. (1978) *Social Origins of Depression* (London: Tavistock).

Buckman, R. (1984) 'Breaking Bad News: Why Is It Still So Difficult?', *British Medical Journal*, vol. 288, no. 1, pp. 1597–9.

Buckman, R. (1998) 'Communication in Palliative Care: A Practical Guide', chapter 4 in D. Doyle *et al.* (eds), *Oxford Textbook of Palliative Medicine*, second edition (Oxford: Oxford Medical Publications, Oxford University Press).

C. (1996) 'Widowed through Suicide', *CRUSE Chronicle*, June, p. 3.

Cambridgeshire County Council (1998) 'Social Services Response to a Disaster', guidance notes for staff; draft for consultation.

Care Sector Consortium (1998) *National Occupational Standards for Care Level Three*, as issued by the Central Statistical Office.

Care Standards Bill (H. L.) (1999) December 1999 (London: HMSO).

Carers (Recognition and Services) Act (1995) (London: HMSO).

Carers National Association (1997) *In on the Act: A Study of Social Services Experiences of the First Year of the Act* (London: Carers National Association).

Cartwright, A. and Seale, C. (1990) *The National History of a Survey: An Account of the Methodological Issues Encouraged in a Study of Life before Death* (London: King's Fund).

Cave, D. (1993) 'Gay and Lesbian Bereavement', in D. Dickenson and M. Johnson (eds), *Death, Dying and Bereavement* (London: Sage).

Cave, D. (1996) 'Good Grief', *Lifeline*, no. 20 (Summer/Autumn), pp. 12–13.

CCETSW (Central Council for Education and Training in Social Work) (1995) *Assuring Quality in the Diploma in Social Work – 1. Rules and Requirements for the Diploma in Social Work* (London: CCETSW).

Chamberlyne, P. (1998) 'Changing Cultures of Care: Underlying Ideologies, Policies and Practices in Post-Communist and Post-Fordist Societies: The Two Germanies', in S. Ramon (ed.), *The Interface between Social Work and Social Policy* (Birmingham: Venture Press).

Cherry, V. (1993) *Grief Experienced*, Friends Fellowship of Healing, reviewed in *CRUSE Chronicle*, February 1995.

Children Act (1989) (c41) (London: HMSO).

Chronicle (1994a) 'Is There Life After death? The Light at the End of the Tunnel', *CRUSE Chronicle*, May, pp. 2–3.

Chronicle (1994b) 'Grief at the Loss of a Loved Daughter', *CRUSE Chronicle*, June, p. 1.

Chronicle (1995) 'Survivor's Guilt', *CRUSE Chronicle*, June, p. 4.

Clark, D. (ed.) (1993a) *The Future for Palliative Care: Issues of Policy and Practice* (Buckingham: Open University Press).

Clark, D. (ed.) (1993b) *The Sociology of Death: Theory, Culture, Practice* (Oxford: Blackwell Publishers).

Cleary, B. (1990) 'The Rainbow Trust: A Domiciliary Crisis Service', in J. Baum, Sr F. Dominica and R. Woodward (eds), *Listen, My Child Has a Lot of Living to Do* (Oxford: Oxford University Press).

Corr, C. (1992) 'A Task-Based Approach to Coping with Dying', *Omega*, vol. 24, no. 2, pp. 81–94.

Couldrick, A. (1995) 'A Cradling of a Different Sort', in S. Smith and M. Pennells (eds), *Interventions with Bereaved Children* (London: Jessica Kingsley Publishers).

Cowles, K. and Rodgers, B. (1993) 'The Concept of Grief: An Evolutionary Perspective', chapter 7 in B. Rodgers and K. Knafl (eds), *Concept Development in Nursing* (Philadelphia: W. B. Saunders Company).

Criminal Justice Act (1991) (London: HMSO).

Currer, A. (1992) 'Allocation of Home Help – a Social Process', unpublished M.Phil. Dissertation, University of Warwick.

Currer, C. (2000) 'Is Grief an Illness?', in J. Hockey *et al.* (eds), *Grief, Mourning and Death Ritual* (Buckingham: Open University Press).

Currer, C. and Stacey, M. (eds) (1986) *Concepts of Health, Illness and Disease: A Comparative Perspective* (Leamington Spa: Berg).

Danbury, H. (1996) *Bereavement Counselling Effectiveness* (Aldershot: Avebury).

David (1999) 'Personal Experience of Loss', *Lifeline*, no. 28, p. 20.

Davidson, K. and Foster, Z. (1995) 'Social Work with Dying and Bereaved Clients: Helping the Workers', *Social Work in Health Care*, vol. 21, no. 4, pp. 1–16.

Davies, R. (1995) 'I Wanted a Pink Coffin', unpublished report of the HIV/AIDS User consultation exercise for Norfolk Social Services, produced by Norfolk County Council Social Services Department.

Davis, A. and Ellis, K. (1995) 'Enforced Altruism in Community Care', in R. Hugman and D. Smith (eds), *Ethical Issues in Social Work* (London: Routledge).

Day, S. (1990) 'Acorns', in J. Baum, Sr F. Dominica and R. Woodward (eds), *Listen, My Child Has a Lot of Living to Do* (Oxford: Oxford University Press).

Dent, A. (1999) 'A New Era in Approaching Children's Grief?', *Lifeline*, no. 28, pp. 13–15.

Dent, A., Condon, L., Blair, P. and Fleming, P. (1996) 'Bereaved Children – Who Cares?', *Health Visitor*, vol. 69, no. 7, pp. 270–1.

Department of Health (1989) *Caring for People*, Cm 849 (London: HMSO).

Department of Health (1995) *A Policy Framework for Commissioning Cancer Services*, a report by the Expert Advisory Group to the Chief Medical Officers of England and Wales (London: Department of Health).

Department of Health (1996) *Personal Social Services Local Authority Statistics* (London: HMSO).

Department of Health (1997) *The New NHS: Modern, Dependable*, Cm 3807 (London: HMSO).

Department of Health (1998) *Modernising Social Services*, Cm 4169 (London: HMSO).

Dickenson, D. and Johnson, M. (1993) *Death, Dying and Bereavement* (London: Sage).

Di Mola, G. (1997) 'Palliative Home Care', chapter 8 in D. Clark, J. Hockley and S. Ahmedzai (eds), *New Themes in Palliative Care* (Buckingham: Open University Press).

Disasters Working Party (1991) *Disasters: Planning for a Caring Response* (London: HMSO).

Dominelli, L. (1997) *Sociology for Social Work* (London: Macmillan).

Douglas, A. and Philpot, T. (1998) *Caring and Coping: A Guide to Social Services* (London: Routledge).

Douglas, I. (1999) 'Reflective Practice', chapter 11 in R. Hogston and P. Simpson (eds), *Foundations of Nursing Practice* (London: Macmillan).

DTI (1999) *Management Best Practice – Social Care* (London: HMSO).

Dyregrov, A. (1991) *Grief in Children* (London: Jessica Kingsley Publishers).

Eisenbruch, M. (1984) 'Ethnic and Cultural Variations in the Development of Bereavement Practices', *Culture, Medicine and Psychiatry*, vol. 8, pp. 315–47.

Eraut, M. (1994) *Developing Professional Knowledge and Competence* (London: The Falmer Press).

European Commission (1998) *Social Protection in Europe 1997* (Luxembourg: Office for Official Publications of the European Communities).

Evans, A. (1994) 'Anticipatory Grief: A Theoretical Challenge', *Palliative Medicine*, vol. 8, pp. 159–65.

Everyman TV programme (1998) 'Surviving Lockerbie', 29 November.

Fahlberg, V. I. (1991) *A Child's Journey Through Placement* (Indianapolis: Perspectives Press).

Fairbairn, G. (1993) 'When a Baby Dies – a Father's View', in D. Dickenson and M. Johnson (eds), *Death, Dying and Bereavement* (London: Sage).

Faulkner, A. (1993) 'Developments in Bereavement Services', in D. Clark (ed.), *The Future for Palliative Care* (Buckingham: Open University Press).

Field, D. (1996) 'Awareness of Modern Dying', *Mortality*, vol. 1, no. 3, pp. 255–65.

Field, D. (1998) 'Special Not Different: General Practitioners' Accounts of Their Care of Dying People', *Social Science and Medicine*, vol. 46, no. 9, pp. 1111–20.

Field, D. and James, N. (1993) 'Where and How People Die', in D. Clark (ed.), *The Future for Palliative Care* (Buckingham: Open University Press).

Field, D., Hockey, J. and Small, N. (1997) *Death, Gender and Ethnicity* (London: Routledge).

Firth, P. (1998) 'A Long-Term Closed Group for Young People', in D. Oliviere, R. Hargreaves and B. Monroe (eds), *Good Practices in Palliative Care* (Aldershot: Ashgate), pp. 86–92.

Firth, S. (1993) 'Approaches to Death in Hindu and Sikh Communities in Britain', in D. Dickenson and M. Johnson (eds), *Death, Dying and Bereavement* (London: Sage).

Fish, D. (1999) *Appreciating Practice in the Caring Professions: Refocusing Professional Development and Practitioner Research* (Oxford: Butterworth Heinemann).

Frankham, J. (1996) 'If you follow the procedures, social workers would be about as much use as chocolate teapots' (Joe, HIV+). A set of case studies of people in East Norfolk living with HIV/AIDS in 1996, unpublished. Norfolk County Council Social Services Department.

Franklin, J. (1989) 'Terminal Care Teams', in T. Philpot (ed.), *Last Things: Social Work with the Dying and Bereaved* (Wallington, Surrey: Reed Business Publishing/Community Care).

Freud, S. (1957) 'Mourning and Melancholia' (1917), in J. Strachey (ed. and trans.), *The Standard Edition of the Complete Psychological Works of Sigmund Freud*, vol. 14, pp. 243–58 (London: Hogarth Press).

Froggatt, K. (1997) 'Rites of Passage and the Hospice Culture', *Mortality*, vol. 2, no. 2, pp. 123–36.

Froggatt, K. (1998) 'Making Sense of Certain Death and Uncertain Dying in Nursing Homes', paper given at Symposium of Social Aspects of Death, Dying and Bereavement, November 1998.

G. (1996) 'Losing a Partner', *CRUSE Chronicle*, May, p. 2.

Gambe, D., Gomes, J., Vijay, K., Rangel, M. and Stubbs, P. (1992) *Improving Practice with Children and Families: A Training Manual* (CCETSW).

George, R. and Sykes, J. (1997) 'Beyond Cancer?', in D. Clark, J. Hockey and S. Ahmedzai (eds), *New Themes in Palliative Care* (Buckingham: Open University Press).

Giddens, A. (1991) *Modernity and Self-Identify: Self and Society in the Late Modern Age* (Cambridge: Polity Press).

Gilliard, J. (1992) 'A Different Kind of Loss', *Social Work Today*, 3 December.

Glaser, B. and Strauss, A. (1965) *Awareness of Dying* (Chicago: Aldine).

Glaser, B. and Strauss, A. (1968) *Time for Dying* (Chicago: Aldine).

Glick, I., Weiss, R. and Parkes, C. M. (1974) *The First Year of Bereavement* (London and New York: John Wiley).

Gorer, G. (1965) *Death, Grief and Mourning in Contemporary Britain* (London: Cresset).

Graham, H. (1983) 'Caring: A Labour of Love', in J. Finch and D. Groves (eds), *A Labour of Love: Women, Work and Caring* (London: Routledge & Kegan Paul).

Grant, G. and Nolan, M. (1993) 'Informal Carers: Sources and Concomitants of Satisfaction', *Health and Social Care*, vol. 1, pp. 147–59.

Gunaratnam, Y. (1997) 'Culture is Not Enough: A Critique of Multi-Culturalism Palliative Care', in D. Field, J. Hockey and N. Small (eds), *Death, Gender and Ethnicity* (London: Routledge).

Hallam, E. (1996) 'Turning the Hourglass: Gender Relations at the Deathbed in Early Modern Canterbury', *Mortality*, vol. 1, no. 1, pp. 61–82.

Hanvey, C. (1989) 'Death in Residence', in T. Philpot (ed.), *Last Things: Social Work with the Dying and Bereaved* (Surrey: Reed Business Publishing/Community Care).

Harrington, R. (1999) 'Unproven Assumptions about the Impact of Bereavement on Children', *Journal of the Royal Society of Medicine*, vol. 92, pp. 230–3.

Harrison, S. (1996) 'Take Two', *Community Care*, 8–14 February.

Hayton, A. (1995) 'Five Steps to Peace', *Lifeline*, no. 18, Summer/Autumn.

Health Act (1999) (c8) (London: HMSO).

Help the Aged (1996) *Bereavement*, advice leaflet.

Hemmings, P. (1991) *All About Me*, a board game (London: Barnardo's publications).

Hemmings, P. (1995) 'Social Work Intervention with Bereaved Children', *Journal of Social Work Practice*, vol. 9, no. 2, pp. 109–30.

Herd, E. (1990) 'Helen House', in J. Baum, Sr F. Dominica, R. Woodward (eds), *Listen, My Child Has a Lot of Living to Do* (Oxford: Oxford University Press).

Hinton, J. (1994) 'Can Home Care Maintain an Acceptable Quality of Life for Patients with Terminal Cancer and Their Relatives?', *Palliative Medicine*, vol. 8, pp. 183–96.

His Holiness the Dalai Lama (Bstan-odzin-rgya-mtsho Dalai Lama XIV) (1962) *My Land and My People* (London: Weidenfeld & Nicolson).

Hockey, J. (1990) *Experiences of Death: An Anthropological Account* (Edinburgh: Edinburgh University Press).

Hogston, R. and Simpson, P. (eds) (1999) *Foundations of Nursing Practice* (London: Macmillan).

Holloway, J. (1990) 'Bereavement Literature: A Valuable Resource for the Bereaved and Those Who Counsel Them', *Interdisciplinary Journal of Pastoral Studies*, vol. 3, pp. 17–26.

Home Office (1994) *Dealing with Disaster*, 2nd edition (London: HMSO).

Hope, V. (1997) 'Constructing Roman Identity: Funerary Monuments and Social Structure in the Roman World', *Mortality*, vol. 2, no. 2, pp. 103–22.

Hospice Information Service (1999) *Directory of Hospice and Palliative Care Services in the U.K. and Republic of Ireland*, edited by A. Jackson and A. Eve for the Hospice Information Service, St Christopher's Hospice, 51–9 Lawrie Park Road, Sydenham, London, SE26 6DU.

d'Houtaud, A. and Field, M. (1986) 'New Research on the Image of Health', in C. Currer and M. Stacey (eds), *Concepts of Health, Illness and Disease* (Leamington Spa: Berg).

Howe, D. (1995) *Attachment Theory for Social Work Practice* (London: Macmillan).

Iliffe, S. (1983) *The NHS – a Picture of Health?* (London: Lawrence & Wishart).

Illich, I. (1976) *Limits to Medicine; Medical Nemesis: The Expropriation of Health* (Harmondsworth: Penguin).

Institute of Actuaries (1998), cited in Henwood, M. (ed.) *Ignored and Invisible? Carers' Experience of the NHS* (London: Carers National Association).

Ironside, V. (1996) *'You'll Get Over It': The Rage of Bereavement* (Harmondsworth, Penguin).

Jack, R. and Mosley, S. (1997) 'The Client Group Preferences of Diploma in Social Work Students: What Are They, Do They Change During Programmes, and What Variables Affect Them?', *British Journal of Social Work*, vol. 27, pp. 893–911.

James, I. A. (1995) 'Helping People with Learning Disabilities to Cope with Bereavement', *British Journal of Learning Disabilities*, vol. 23, pp. 74–8.

Jenkinson, K. and Bodkin, C. (1996) 'Sudden Death – a Personal Journey', *Lifeline*, vol. 19, Winter/Spring, pp. 12–14.

Jennings, W. (1997) 'My Heart Will Go On', love theme from the film *Titanic*, Famous Music Corporation, T. C. Music Publishing Inc, Ensign Music Corporation, Fox Film Music corporation and Blue Sky Rider Songs.

Jewett, C. (1984) *Helping Children Cope with Separation and Loss* (London: Batsford with BAAF).

Jonker, G. (1997) 'The Many Facets of Islam: Death, Dying and Disposal between Orthodox Rule and Historical Convention', in C. M. Parkes, P. Laungani and B. Young (eds), *Death and Bereavement across Cultures* (London: Routledge).

Katz, J. (1993) 'Jewish Perspectives on Death, Dying and Bereavement', in D. Dickenson and M. Johnson (eds), *Death, Dying and Bereavement* (London: Sage).

Katz, J. and Sidell, M. (1994) *Easeful Death: Caring for Dying and Bereaved People* (London: Hodder & Stoughton).

Klass, D., Silverman P. R. and Nickman, S. L. (1996) *Continuing Bonds: New Understandings of Grief* (Philadelphia: Taylor & Francis).

Kohner, N. (1993) 'The Loss of a Baby: Parents' Needs and Professional Practice After Early Loss', in D. Dickenson and M. Johnson (eds), *Death, Dying and Bereavement* (London: Sage).

Kubler-Ross, E. (1970) *On Death and Dying* (London: Tavistock).

Laing and Buisson (1995) *Care Guide* (London).

Lamb, D. (1991) 'Definitions of Death', in *Salute, Malattia, Morte India ed Europa a Confronto*, Istituto Veneto di Scienze, Lettere ed Arti Associatzione Italia-India di Venezia (Proceedings of Conference).

Lancet, The (1997) 'From What Will We Die in 2020?', editorial, *The Lancet*, vol. 349, no. 9061, p. 1263.

Lewis, J. with Bernstock, P., Bovell, V. and Wookey, F. (1997) 'Implementing Care Management: Issues in Relation to the New Community Care', *British Journal of Social Work*, vol. 27, pp. 5–24.

Lifeline (1999) Summer 1999, no. 28, pp. 11–19. Responses to Professor Richard Harrington.

Lindemann, E. (1944) 'Symptomatology and Management of Acute Grief', *American Journal of Psychiatry*, vol. 101, pp. 141–8.

Lister, L. (1991) 'Men and Grief: A Review of Research', *Smith College Studies in Social Work*, vol. 61, pp. 220–35.

Littlewood, J. (1993) 'The Denial of Death and Rites of Passage in Contemporary Societies', in D. Clark (ed.), *The Sociology of Death* (Oxford: Blackwell).

Lloyd, M. (1997) 'Dying and Bereavement, Spirituality and Social Work in a Market Economy of Welfare', *British Journal of Social Work*, vol. 27, pp. 175–90.

Lofland, L. H. (1978) *The Craft of Dying: The Modern Face of Death* (London and Beverly Hills: Sage).

Lorenz, W. (1994) *Social Work in a Changing Europe* (London: Routledge).

Maguire, P. and Faulkner, A. (1988) 'Improve the Counselling Skills of Doctors and Nurses in Cancer Care', *British Medical Journal*, vol. 297, no. 2, pp. 907–9.

Maliphant, L. (1996) 'Bereavement Groupwork with People with Learning Disabilities', *Lifeline*, 20, Summer/Autumn.

Marris, P. (1958) *Widows and Their Families* (London: Routledge & Kegan Paul).

Marris, P. (1982) 'Attachment and Society', in C. M. Parkes and J. Stevenson-Hinde (eds), *The Place of Attachment in Human Behaviour* (London: Tavistock).

Marris, P. (1986) *Loss and Change*, revised edition (London: Routledge).

Marris, P. (1991) 'The Social Construction of Uncertainty', in C. M. Parkes, J. Stevenson-Hinde and P. Marris, *Attachment Across the Life Cycle* (London: Routledge).

Marsh, P. and Triselotis, J. (1996) 'Social Workers: Their Training and First Year in Work', in N. Connelly (ed.), *Training Social Services Staff: Evidence from New Research*, report of a conference, Research in Social Work Education, no. 4 (London: National Institute for Social Work).

McLaren, J. (1995) 'The Loss of a Child', *CRUSE Chronicle*, June, pp. 1–2.

McLaren, J. (1997) Editorial, *Lifeline*, no. 22, Spring.

McLaughlin, J. (1994) Postbag, *CRUSE Chronicle*, October.

Mead, C. (1996) *Journeys of Discovery: Creative Learning from Disaster* (London: National Institute for Social Work).

Mental Health Act 1983 (c20) (London: HMSO).

Monroe, B. (1998) 'Social Work in Palliative Care', chapter 13 in D. Doyle, G. Hanks and N. MacDonald (eds), *The Oxford Handbook of Palliative Medicine*, second edition (Oxford: Oxford University Press).

Monroe, B. (1999) 'Supporting Bereaved Children: Where Are We? Where Should We Be?', paper given to annual conference of NABS, Nottingham, June 1999.

Moore, O. (1996) *PWA – Looking AIDS in the Face* (London: Picador).

Moore, S. (1993) *Social Welfare Alive!* (Cheltenham: Stanley Thornes).

Mr G. J. (1996) Postbag, *CRUSE Chronicle*, March.

Mrs G. M. (1997/8) 'A Deeper Perspective', *CRUSE Chronicle*, Dec/Jan, p. 4.

Mrs J. B. (1994/5) Postbag, *CRUSE Chronicle*, Dec/Jan.

Mrs J. T. (1994) 'Reflections on Bereavement', *CRUSE Chronicle*, May.

Mrs R. (1996) Postbag, *CRUSE Chronicle*, May.

Mrs S. T. (1995) 'My Father', *CRUSE Chronicle*, March.

Mulkay, M. and Ernst, J. (1991) 'The Changing Profile of Social Death', *Archives of European Sociology*, vol. 32, pp. 172–96.

National Association of Bereavement Services (NABS) (1999) Membership Information and Annual Report.

National Council for Hospice and Specialist Palliative Care Services (1995) *Specialist Palliative Care: A Statement of Definitions*, Occasional Paper No. 8, London, October.

National Funerals College (1998) *The Dead Citizens Charter, A Citizens Charter for the Dead*, the complete edition. Copies from The National Funerals College, 3 Priory Road, Clifton, Bristol, BS8 1TX, tel: 017 928 9023.

National Health Service and Community Care Act 1990 (c19) (London: HMSO).

Newburn, T. (1993) *Disaster and After* (London: Jessica Kingsley Publishers).

Newburn, T. (1996) 'Some Lessons from Hillsborough', in C. Mead (ed.), *Journeys of Discovery: Creative Learning from Disaster* (London: National Institute for Social Work).

Nuttall, M. (1994/5) 'Loss in Later Life: On the Death of a Spouse', *Lifeline*, no. 16.

Office for National Statistics (2000) 1998 *Vital Statistics: Mortality (Registrations), England and Wales, using mid-1997 population estimates.* ©Crown Copyright.

Oliviere, D., Hargreaves, R. and Monroe, B. (1998) *Good Practices in Palliative Care* (Aldershot: Ashgate).

Open University (1999) *Death and Dying*, K260, Workbook 2 'Caring for Dying People', p. 13.

Oswin, M. (1990) 'The Grief that Does Not Speak', *Search*, Winter, pp. 45–7.

Parkes, C. M. (1970) 'The First Year of Bereavement: A Longitudinal Study of the Reaction of London Widows to the Death of Their Husbands', *Psychiatry*, vol. 33, p. 444.

Parkes, C. M. (1980) 'Bereavement Counselling: Does It Work?', *British Medical Journal*, 5 July, pp. 3–6.

Parkes, C. M. (1981) 'Evaluation of a Bereavement Service', *Journal of Preventive Psychiatry*, vol. 1, pp. 179–88.

Parkes, C. M. (1987) 'Bereavement', in *The Oxford Companion to the Mind* (Oxford: Oxford University Press).

Parkes, C. M. (1993) 'Bereavement as a Psycho-social Transition: Processes of Adaptation to Change', chapter 6 in M. Stroebe, W. Stroebe and R. Hansson (eds), *Handbook of Bereavement* (Cambridge: Cambridge University Press).

Parkes, C. M. (1996) *Bereavement*, 3rd edition (London: Routledge). (First published 1972; 3rd edition published in paperback by Penguin 1998.)

Parkes, C. M., Laungani, P. and Young, B. (1997) *Death and Bereavement Across Cultures* (London: Routledge).

Parkes, C. M. and Stevenson-Hinde, J. (1982) *The Place of Attachment in Human Behaviour* (London: Tavistock).

Parkes, C. M., Stevenson-Hinde, J. and Marris, P. (1991) *Attachment Across the Life Cycle* (London: Routledge).

Parkes, C. M. and Weiss, R. S. (1983) *Recovery from Bereavement* (New York: Basic Books).

Partington, M. (1996) 'Salvaging the Sacred', *The Guardian Weekend*, 18 May, pp. 14–23.

Parton, N. (1996) *Social Theory, Social Change and Social Work* (London: Routledge).

Pearson, M. (1986) 'Racist Notions of Ethnicity and Culture in Health Education', in S. Rodmell and A. Watt (eds), *The Politics of Health Education* (London: Routledge & Kegan Paul).

Pennells, M. and Smith, S. (1995) *The Forgotten Mourners* (London: Jessica Kingsley Publishers).

Philpot, T. (ed.) (1989) *Last Things. Social Work with the Dying and Bereaved* (Surrey: Reed Business Publishing/Community Care).

Picardie, R. (1998) *Before I Say Goodbye* (London: Penguin).

Poulos, S. (1996–7) 'Letters to Gil – a Mother's Journey through Grief', *Lifeline*, nos 19, 20, 21, 22.

Quinn, A. (1998) 'Learning from Palliative Care: Concepts to Underpin the Transfer of Knowledge from Specialist Palliative Care to Mainstream Social Work Settings', *Social Work Education*, vol. 17, no. 1, pp. 9–19.

Ramon, S. (1997) 'Building Resistance through Training', *Breakthrough*, vol. 1, no. 1, pp. 57–64.

Raphael, B. (1984) *The Anatomy of Bereavement* (London: Routledge).

Read, S. (1998) 'The Palliative Care Needs of People with Learning Disabilities', *British Journal of Community Nursing*, vol. 3, no. 7, pp. 356–61.

Registered Homes Act 1984 (London: HMSO).

Relf, M. (1995) 'Bereavement', in R. Twycross (ed.), *Introducing Palliative Care* (Oxford: Radcliffe).

Relf, M. (1997) 'How Effective are Volunteers in Providing Bereavement Care?', in Proceedings of the Fourth Congress of the European Association for Palliative Care, Barcelona, 6–9 December 1995.

Riches, G. and Dawson, P. (1997) 'Shoring Up the Walls of Heartache: Parental Responses to the Death of a Child', in D. Field, J. Hockey and N. Small (eds), *Death, Gender and Ethnicity* (London: Routledge).

Rickford, F. (1992) 'Toxic Shock', *Social Work Today*, 3 December 1992, pp. 16–17.

Rosenblatt, P. C. (1993) 'Cross-Cultural Variation in the Experience, Expression and Understanding of Grief', in D. P. Irish *et al.* (eds), *Ethnic Variations in Dying, Death and Grief: Diversity in Universality* (London: Taylor & Francis).

Rosenblatt, P. C. (1997) 'Grief in Small-Scale Societies', in C. M. Parkes, P. Laungani and B. Young (eds), *Death and Bereavement Across Cultures* (London: Routledge).

Rosenblatt, P. C., Walsh, R. P. and Jackson, D. (1976) *Grief and Mourning in a Cross-Cultural Perspective* (Washington D. C: HRAF Press).

Rugg, J. (1998) '"A Few Remarks on Modern Sepulture": Current Trends and New Direction in Cemetery Research', *Mortality*, vol. 3, no. 2, pp. 111–21.

Saarl, C. (1997) 'Finding a WAY Forward', *Lifeline*, no. 23, Summer, pp. 24–9.

Seale, C. (1991) 'Death from Cancer and Death from Other Causes: The Relevance of the Hospice Approach', *Palliative Medicine*, vol. 5, pp. 12–19.

Seale, C. (1993) 'Demographic Change and the Case of the Dying 1969–1987', in D. Dickenson and M. Johnson (eds), *Death, Dying and Bereavement* (London: Sage).

Seale, C. (1995) 'Dying Alone', *Sociology of Health and Illness*, vol. 17, no. 3, pp. 376–92.

Seale, C. (1996) 'Living Alone Towards the End of Life', *Ageing and Society*, vol. 16, pp. 75–91.

Seale, C. (1998) *Constructing Death: The Sociology of Dying and Bereavement* (Cambridge: Cambridge University Press).

Seale, C. and Addington-Hall, J. (1994) 'Euthanasia: Why People Want to Die Earlier', *Social Science and Medicine*, vol. 39, no. 5, pp. 647–54.

Seale, C., Addington-Hall, J. and McCarthy, M. (1997) 'Awareness of Dying: Prevalence, Causes and Consequences', *Social Science and Medicine*, vol. 45, no. 3, pp. 477–84.

Searle, Y. and Streng, I. (1996) *The Grief Game* (London: Jessica Kingsley Publishers).

Seymour, C. (1997) 'Bereavement', paper given at Primary Care and Mental Health Services Workshop, 16 April 1997.

Shee, V. (1996) 'A Teenager's Personal Testimony', *Lifeline*, no. 19, Winter/Spring, p. 18.

Sheldon, F. (1995) 'Home Coming', Inside Special Supplement on Terminal Illness, *Community Care*, 26 January–1 February, p. 1.

Sheldon, F. (1997) *Psychosocial Palliative Care* (Cheltenham: Stanley Thornes).

Sheldon, F. (1998) 'Education for Social Workers', in D. Doyle, G. W. Hanks and N. MacDonald (eds), *The Oxford Textbook of Palliative Medicine*, second edition (Oxford: Oxford University Press).

Shemmings, Y. (1996) *Death, Dying and Residential Care* (Aldershot: Avebury).

Siddell, M., Katz, J. and Komaromy, C. (1998) 'Death and Dying in Residential and Nursing Homes for Older People: Examining the Case for Palliative Care', unpublished report of research, The Open University.

Simpson, M. (1987) *Dying, Death and Grief: A Critical Bibliography* (University of Philadelphia Press).

Slater, P. and Oliviere, D. (1997) 'Social Work and Palliative Care: An Integrated Approach', *Journal of Practice and Staff Development* (January), vol. 5, no. 4, pp. 53–7.

Smith, C. R. (1982*) Social Work with the Dying and Bereaved* (London: Macmillan).

Smith, D. (1993) 'The Terminally Ill Patient's Right to be in Denial', *Omega*, vol. 27, no. 2, pp. 115–21.

Smith, S. C. and Pennells, M. (1995) *Interventions with Bereaved Children* (London: Jessica Kingsley Publishers).

Staudacher, C. (1991) *Men and Grief* (Oakland: New Harbinger Publications Inc.)

St Christopher's Hospice (1998) 'Candle; Children, Young People and Loss', Service leaflet.

Stein, A. and Woolley, H. (1990) 'An Evaluation of Hospice Care for Children', in J. Baum, Sr F. Dominica and R. Woodward (eds), *Listen, My Child Has a Lot of Living to Do* (Oxford: Oxford University Press).

Stockwin, J. (1995) 'Death of a Son', *CRUSE Chronicle*, February.

Stokes, J. and Crossley, D. (1995) 'Camp Winston – a Residential Intervention for Bereaved Children', in S. Smith and M. Pennells (eds), *Interventions with Bereaved Children* (London: Jessica Kingsley Publishers).

Strauss, A. L., Corbin, J., Fagerhaugh, D., Glaser, B., Maines, D., Suczek, B. and Weiner, C. (1984) *Chronic Illness and the Quality of Life* (St Louis: Mosby).

Stroebe, M. (1992) 'Coping with Bereavement: A Review of the Group Work Hypothesis', *Omega*, vol. 26, no. 1, pp. 19–42.

Stroebe, M. (1997) 'From Mourning and Melancholia to Bereavement and Biography: An Assessment of Walter's New Model of Grief', *Mortality*, vol. 2, no. 3, pp. 255–62.

Stroebe, M. (1998) 'New Directions in Bereavement Research: Exploration of Gender Differences', *Palliative Medicine*, vol. 12, pp. 5–12.

Stroebe, M. and Schut, H. (1995) 'The Dual Process/Model of Coping with Loss', paper presented at the International Work Group on Death, Dying and Bereavement, St Catherine's College, Oxford, 26–29 June 1995.

Stroebe, M. and Schut, H. (1998) 'Culture and Grief', *Bereavement Care*, vol. 17, no. 1, pp. 7–11.

Stroebe, M. and Schut, H. (1999) 'The Dual Process Model of Coping with Bereavement: Rationale and Description', *Death Studies*, vol. 23, pp. 197–224.

Stroebe, M. and Stroebe, W. (1987) *Bereavement and Health* (Cambridge: Cambridge University Press).

Stroebe, M. and Stroebe, W. (1991) 'Does "Grief Work" Work?', *Journal of Counselling and Clinical Psychology*, vol. 59, no. 3, pp. 479–82.

Stroebe, M., Stroebe, W. and Hansson, R. (eds) (1993) *Handbook of Bereavement: Theory, Research and Intervention* (Cambridge: Cambridge University Press).

Stuart, S. (1994) 'Widowed Young', *CRUSE Chronicle*, October, pp. 1–2.

Sudnow, D. (1967) *Passing On: The Social Organisation of Dying* (Englewood Cliffs, NJ: Prentice-Hall).

Sutcliffe, P., Tufnell, G. and Cornish, U. (1998) *Working with the Dying and Bereaved* (London: Macmillan).

Sweeting, H. and Gilhooly, M. (1997) 'Dementia and the Phenomenon of Social Death', *Sociology of Health and Illness*, vol. 19, no. 1, pp. 93–117.

Tebbutt, C. (1994) 'After Suicide', *CRUSE Chronicle*, July/August, pp. 3–4.

Thomas, J. (1995) 'The Effects on the Family of Miscarriage, Termination for Abnormality, Stillbirth and Neonatal Death', *Child: Care, Health and Development*, vol. 21, no. 6, pp. 413–23.

Thompson, A. (1999) 'High Anxiety', *Community Care*, 1–7 April, pp. 18–19.

Thompson, N. (1997a) *Anti-Discriminatory Practice*, 2nd edition (London: Macmillan).

Thompson, N. (1997b) 'Masculinity and Loss', in D. Field, J. Hockey and N. Small (eds), *Death, Gender and Ethnicity* (London: Routledge).

Thornes, R. (1988) *Care of Dying Children and Their Families*, Report of working party, National Association of Health Authorities, Birmingham.

Thornes, R. (1990) 'Towards a Comprehensive System of Care for Dying Children and Their Families', in J. Baum, Sr F. Dominica and R. Woodward (eds), *Listen, My Child Has a Lot of Living to Do* (Oxford: Oxford University Press).

Timmermans, S. (1994) 'Dying of Awareness: The Theory of Awareness Contexts Revisited', *Sociology of Health and Illness*, vol. 16, no. 3, pp. 322–39.

Timmermans, S. (1998) 'Social Death as Self-Fulfilling Prophecy: David Sudnow's *Passing On* Revisited', *The Sociological Quarterly*, vol. 39, no. 3, pp. 453–72.

Todd, R. (1994) 'Aftermath of a Road Accident', *CRUSE Chronicle*, September.

Townsend, J., Frank, A. O., Fermont, D., Dyer, S., Karran, O. and Walgrave, A. (1990) 'Terminal Cancer and Patients' Preference for Place of Death', *British Medical Journal*, vol. 301, pp. 415–17.

Tumelty, D. (1990) *Social Work in the Wake of Disaster* (London: Jessica Kingsley Publishers).

Turner, V. W. (1969) *The Ritual Process* (Harmondsworth: Penguin).

Twigg, J. (1989) 'Models of Carers: How Do Social Care Agencies Conceptualise Their Relationship with Informal Carers?', *Journal of Social Policy*, vol. 18, no. 1, pp. 53–66.

Tyndall, N. (1993) *Counselling in the Voluntary Sector* (Buckingham: Open University Press).

van Gennep, A. (1960) *The Rites of Passage* (London: Routledge & Kegan Paul).

Victor, C. (1993) 'Health Policy and Services for Dying People and Their Carers', in D. Dickenson and M. Johnson (eds), *Death, Dying and Bereavement* (London: Sage).

Walter, T. (1994) *The Revival of Death* (London: Routledge).

Walter, T. (1996) 'A New Model of Grief: Bereavement and Biography', *Mortality*, vol. 1, no. 1, pp. 7–25.

Walter, T. (1997a) 'Letting Go and Keeping Hold: A Reply to Stroebe', *Mortality*, vol. 2, no. 3, pp. 263–5.

Walter, T. (1997b) Book review, *Mortality*, vol. 2, no. 2 (July), pp. 173–4.

Walter, T. (1999) *On Bereavement* (Buckingham: Open University Press).

Ward, B. (1993) *Good Grief: Exploring Feelings, Loss and Death with Under Elevens: A Holistic Approach* (London: Jessica Kingsley Publishers).

Warren, B. (1993) *Using the Creative Arts in Therapy*, 2nd edition (London: Routledge).

Weiss, R. (1991) 'The Attachment Bond in Childhood and Adulthood', in C. M. Parkes, J. Stevenson-Hinde and P. Marris (eds), *Attachment Across the Life Cycle* (London: Routledge).

Whistler, L. (1987) *The Initials in the Heart* (London: Weidenfeld & Nicolson).

Wikan, U. (1988) 'Bereavement and Loss in Two Muslim Communities: Egypt and Bali Compared', *Social Science and Medicine*, vol. 27, no. 5, pp. 451–60.

Williams, M. (1998) 'Listening to Men's Voices in Palliative Care', in D. Oliviere, R. Hargreaves and B. Monroe (eds), *Good Practices in Palliative Care* (Aldershot: Ashgate).

Woodward, R. (1990) 'The Cancer and Leukaemia in Childhood Trust (CLIC)', in J. Baum, Sr F. Dominica and R. Woodward (eds), *Listen, My Child Has a Lot of Living to Do* (Oxford: Oxford University Press).

Woolfenden, J. (1997) 'Open Space: A Bereavement and Loss Group in a Closed Women's Prison', *Psychodynamic Counselling*, vol. 3, no. 1 (February), pp. 77–82.

Worden, W. (1991) *Grief Counselling and Grief Therapy – a Handbook for the Mental Health Practitioner*, 2nd edition (London: Routledge). (1st edition published in Great Britain in 1983 by Tavistock.)

Worden, W. (1996) *Children and Grief* (London and New York: The Guilford Press).

Wortman, C. B. and Silver, R. C. (1989) 'The Myths of Coping with Loss', *Journal of Consulting and Clinical Psychology*, vol. 57, pp. 349–57.

Young, M. and Cullen, L. (1996) *A Good Death* (London: Routledge).

Index